The Beyond26 Story

How Community Based Employment for Individuals with Disabilities Changes Lives

By Dirk Bakhuyzen

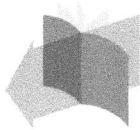

Chapbook Press

Schuler Books
2660 28th Street SE
Grand Rapids, MI 49512
(616) 942-7330
www.schulerbooks.com

The Beyond26 Story

ISBN 13: 9781957169064 (paperback)

ISBN 13: 9781957169088 (eBook)

Library of Congress Control Number: 2022907496 (paperback edition)

Printed in the United States by Chapbook Press.

Acknowledgements

When I reflect on writing this book, the whole story begins with an idea sparked by my son Kyle and the Holy Spirit. In a world where we ask God for breakthrough answers in our life, God has done just that in my life! Our life story since 2006 would not have happened without that prodding and prompting. God took our family and created a journey I could never have imaged. Thank You Lord for walking with us every day.

I could not have done it without my spouse. Phyllis has walked every step with me and lived through the years Will was not as content as he is now. Who would have thought adopting a 9-year-old special needs son at the ages of 51 and 48 would have become this remarkable? Thank you, Phyllis, for walking this journey with me, I love you.

My Board of Directors at Beyond26 has been with me since the very beginning. Bob and Vicki Wondergem, sister Mary Van Oeveren, niece Jenn Bakhuyzen, Ellie VanKeulen, Gary Courtright, Ed and Kyle Beuche, and Leon Lynn, thank you for the round table beginning (at Russ' restaurant) and supporting my enthusiasm for the past 5 years.

My team at Beyond26- Emily, Elisa, Nick, Ellie, Andrea, Carla, Pam, Marie, Merri, Lyn and all the selfless volunteers that help us each week, thank you for your dedication to our jobseekers!

When I first wrote the basic story it was just a story. When I asked writer Lorilee Crater to help me, she brought the book to life. Thank you so much for all the interviews, questions, and stories you brought to life in the book. I appreciate your talent and writer's expertise!

To all the business partners, donors, volunteers, and jobseekers of Beyond26. These stories all spun out of your relationship with me and our staff. Thanks for supporting us, encouraging me, and creating such wonderful work environments. At the time of this writing, we have placed 101 jobseekers in jobs around West Michigan. Hats off to all of you!

My family has been so supportive since the beginning. Thanks for loving on our jobseekers in the document shredding facility. Thanks for encouraging me to spread the news and help others start their version of Beyond26. "Putting Faith to Work", it is the right thing for all communities!

Dirk Bakhuyzen

CHAPTER 1

The Start of It All

It was just an ordinary Sunday, until it became extraordinary.

"Hey mom and dad, we should adopt him!" Kyle said, pointing to a magazine from Bethany Christian Services, an adoption agency based in Grand Rapids, Michigan, where we live. We were about to sit down to Sunday lunch.

"Adopt who?" Phyllis said, busying herself with laying platters of meat and bowls of potatoes and vegetables on the table.

"This boy that has Down Syndrome in the Bethany newsletter," said Kyle. Phyllis didn't miss a beat. "Nope, we've been there and done that," she said, passing the potatoes. That case, it seemed, was closed. At least it sure appeared to be so. But that tiny seed, planted by Kyle, would quickly take root in all our hearts. After the kids left the table following Sunday dinner, I picked up the newsletter and found the young man Kyle was referring to. His name was Will.

***

Phyllis and I got married when I was twenty-one and she was nineteen. We wasted no time in starting our family; by the time of our first anniversary, we were pregnant with our son, Dirk III. Even though we were very young, we were able to sock away money for a down payment on a house. It helped that the landlord of the apartment we lived in offered us a deal: keep the hallways clean and you can offset your rent. We did the cleaning for him and paid $75 per month for the year we lived there. Phyllis was also working at that time, which also helped cover our expenses. It was 1978, and interest rates were 14%. Yes, you read that right. So even though our expenses were low, and we had two incomes coming in, we still needed a boost. *Maybe we'll find someone willing to do a land contract*, we thought. And we did. An older woman in a neighborhood called Alger Heights on the Southeast side of Grand Rapids was willing to sell us her little two-bedroom bungalow on a land contract. The house was $26,000 and she charged us 9% interest. Three years later, we moved a couple of streets over into a three-bedroom bungalow.

We began living our American dream. Our second son, Josh, and third son, Kyle, followed with approximately two years between each. It was not long after Kyle was born, Phyllis required a partial hysterectomy, which eliminated our ability to have any more biological children. Three children is a good number for most people, but something in our spirits told us we were not done having children. And Phyllis longed for a girl. It was not long after having our third son, Kyle, that Phyllis said she would really like to adopt a daughter. "Three strikes, you're out," Phyllis joked to me. "Let's adopt!"

Before we were married, we had talked about adopting children. Phyllis's older brother and sister already had adopted through Bethany Christian Services. We decided that if ever the opportunity presented itself, we would strongly consider adoption. Adoption was part of our plan from the onset of our lives together.

When we were adopting Leah, Phyllis's oldest brother and sister-in-law were also adopting siblings from Korea, but they didn't want to steal Phyllis's thunder in *her* first adoption. After Leah came home to us, they said, "Oh, by the way, we have siblings coming from Korea soon too." Korea was the place for us, I guess.

With the guidance of Bethany Christian Services, we decided to adopt internationally from Korea. The agency's strongest program was in Korea, and we were told more girls are adopted from Korea than boys. At that time, they could not guarantee a girl placement for us, but they did say it seemed likely we would get a girl. This began what I call our longest pregnancy. We had our church family praying with us and as the months went by, we were constantly being asked, 'have you heard anything?' After a little over two years, we were asked if we would consider a girl that a different family had recently rejected. They rejected her because she had a small head size which they felt was indicative of cognitive problems. We had no such qualms and immediately fell in love with this eight-month little girl when we first looked at the photos Bethany sent us. She was our daughter, instantly. Leah had a hard life before she came to us. Not only had she been left in front of a police station, but she had also sustained severe burns along the way. We will probably never know how she got those burns.

In July of 1986 we were met at the airport with our daughter Leah Elaine-Song. (With Korean adoptions, it was an option to not travel to one's child's birth country but to instead have your child accompanied on the airplane by caring individuals hired by the adoption agency.) At first, she gravitated to me for the most part, clinging to me. I fed her scrambled eggs on one of the first mornings, and we realized later that she had left those eggs in her mouth, probably worrying that she didn't know where her next meal was coming from. Fairly quickly though, she began to swallow her food and grow in trust. This Korean toddler who had heard only Korean and even spoke a little bit of her native language learned English. She discovered that she would be fed regularly and taken care of with a consistency she likely had never known.

When Leah came to live with us, our snug house on Paris Street became too small for our family. We decided to move into the Godfrey Lee neighborhood of Grand Rapids, to a bigger house on Cleveland Street. Now it is almost entirely a Hispanic neighborhood, but in those days, it was a mix of ethnicities. Over time our family became a unit. It helped that Leah was and is a bundle of joy who bursts out laughing over most life events! Kyle became her protector and "go to" big brother. Life was and is good, every day. Leah went on to receive a bachelor's degree in Graphic Design and served in the Army National Guard with an honorable discharge. She now works fulltime for her brothers in their landscaping and tree service businesses. We could not be prouder of her accomplishments.

Leah would also become a key figure in our adoption of Will and his future. We just didn't know that yet.

CHAPTER 2

A Breakthrough of the Heart

When Kyle first mentioned Will's name at Sunday dinner, it had been nineteen years since we had adopted Leah. We were definitely *done*—done! The whole incident flew out of my head until the next Bethany newsletter came in the mail and Kyle reiterated the same statement. "You guys should adopt Will," he said. "Will is still in there." He was referring to the updated newsletter, which featured orphans available for adoption and needing homes. Sure enough, there was the picture of Will, posing with his beaming smile and both hands in the air, his fingers giving the victory sign.

Phyllis was unmoved. "We've been there and done that Kyle!" she answered in a downbeat tone. Her resolve was established, and there seemed to be no wiggle room for this idea. However, my heart began to open. I can't explain how or why, but it was happening. I was fifty-one and Phyllis was forty-eight when we started the process. My children were all in their twenties, with the youngest being Leah at age twenty-one. We were empty nesters. We had done some traveling and hoped to do more. Why on earth would we upend our lives this way? Humanly speaking, we didn't have a leg to stand on. It made no rational sense. Yet God's ways are not our ways. My heart was mysteriously softening to this crazy idea. *I have the heart capacity to do this again*, I thought to myself. *We have the financial resources to support this child.* My heart was stirring in a way I could not explain.

***

Three months later, the Bethany Christian Services newsletter came again, and Kyle did not take long to make his now familiar statement.

"Hey, Mom and Dad, Will is still in the newsletter, seriously, you should adopt him!"

Phyllis was annoyed and direct: "Kyle, knock it off"! I had already checked, secretly, and knew Will was still in the newsletter. I looked for him the day we received it.

The next day I asked Phyllis whether she would consider adopting again. Her answer surprised me. "Dirk, we are too old. They would never consider us!" So, the door *was* open a tiny bit! I could work with that. My wife did not *completely* shut the idea down. I asked if it would be alright to call our niece, Alison, who worked at Bethany Christian Services in their international adoption department. Phyllis approved so the next morning I called Alison.

"Hi, Uncle Dirk!" Alison said in her in her usual chipper voice. "What going on?" When I asked whether Phyllis and I were too old to adopt again, Alison asked what type of adoption I was talking about. When I mentioned the young man "Will" in the newsletter she paused a couple seconds. "I gave him that name," she said. "Bethany cannot use real names in our newsletters, so we choose names. I chose that name!" (The fact that our niece named our son before any of us knew he would be our son is just another example of God being in the details.)

Alison continued. "So, the answer to your question Uncle Dirk, is you are not too old to adopt," she said. "We look for parents with experience and patience to adopt a child with disabilities." I pushed Phyllis's slightly open door a bit more, and the conversation started at our house in earnest. Should we adopt a nine-year-old boy with Down Syndrome? Before starting the process, we had to know and be reassured that this was Gods will for our lives.

Phyllis and I decided that we would think, pray, and wait on God to give a clear indication this was right for us. We chose to give it six weeks.

At the beginning of week two, I was at my basement desk reading my Bible and I came to James 1:27: "Religion that God our Father accepts as pure and faultless is this: to look after orphans and widows in their distress and to keep oneself from being polluted by the world." After reading it a couple times I charged up the stairs and excitedly showed Phyllis what I read.

"This is confirmation for me, Phyllis! I don't need any more time, this is my path, I want to adopt Will!"

Phyllis was not as blown away as I was. "Haven't you read that verse before?" she asked. "That is a well-known adoption verse, I am surprised you have not read that before today. And besides, I still need the full six weeks. I am not committed or sure."

That was a long six weeks for all of us. I tried to be patient, but as the weeks wore on, I grew anxious for an answer from Phyllis. We had already talked through the pros and cons. What worried me was the cons seemed to be winning.

The cons: I was fifty-two years old, and Phyllis was forty-eight. Since Will was nine years old, we would be sixty seven and sixty four before he aged out of the school system. If we set a goal of Will living in at a group home by age thirty, we would both be over seventy years old. Responsibility for this young man would be ours until we died. It seemed overwhelming to say the least. But there were some items on the pro column, too.

The pros: we would be giving an orphan with a disability a loving home. We had the energy and financial resources to see this through. We were and are homebodies that do not need to be on the go. We would be answering a call to care for the orphan. We have love to give. And you know what the Bible says about love: "And now these three things remain: faith, hope and love. But the greatest of these is love." 1 Corinthians 13:13 (NIV)

Then Phyllis' heart began to open. Her faith is strong, but she was not fully convinced we were up to the challenge. She had a lot of anxiety and fear about what the future would hold for us. Her fear was that much of the responsibility would fall on her since I worked outside the home. It was a truth that I could not deny (even though I tried!). We prayed through these challenges, and Phyllis came to a point of being okay with the idea but with reservations.

To be honest, she wasn't totally convinced at the end of the six weeks. She still had her doubts that this could all work out. We would be in our sixties and have a child who still depended on us. What if we got sick or couldn't care for him properly? We mapped out what his life and ours would look like when he was twenty-six, and we were in our late sixties.

Twenty-six is the magic number when young adults with disabilities age out of school. You see, fifty years ago at the time of this writing, in 1971, Dr. Charles Mange wrote our state's special education law that mandates an education for children and young adults with disabilities to age twenty-six. I believe Michigan is the only state in the nation that believes in educating every child to his or her maximum potential from babyhood to age twenty-six.

Being from Michigan, we are more fortunate than most parents of young adults with disabilities. Phyllis and I planned for the eventuality that by age twenty-six, Will would go to live in a group home where he could find some independence from us, become employed and find a pattern of life he could enjoy. We didn't know as much then as we do now, but our goals for him are the same: We want our son to be employed and happy with his routine.

Phyllis and I talked to our children and asked if they would take care of Will if something happened to us. They agreed that they would, which was a crucial commitment on their part. We could not have moved forward without this safety net in place.

Fifteen years later, God has taken care of so many things that we were afraid of. Leah now lives at home with us and has agreed to be Will's caregiver when we are no longer able. Sister and brother are very good together, and Phyllis and I can take vacations together knowing Will is well cared for.

But back in 2006, all we knew is that we were going to move forward in faith over fear. We decided to adopt a nine-year-old boy from Hong Kong. Our son Will was coming home.

CHAPTER 3

Bringing Will Home

How does a heart open to love a child that is not your own? How exactly does that happen? A child who was rejected by his biological parents and has Down Syndrome? It is a quirky question because it has a quirky answer. God gifts certain people to be able take a child or young adult into their home and love them like they do their biological children. I know from experience that the love I hold for Leah and Will is the same as the love I feel for my biological children.

Will was adopted as an older child, not as a toddler like his sister Leah. The love we have for him put us in a vulnerable position because we did not know if the love would be reciprocated. The only explanation is faith. We had faith that all our children would recognize and respond to the true emotion and love we had for them. Faith that as our efforts would solidify, our intent and trust would begin and build. Faith that eventually they would love us back to complete the connection. And they did.

***

Leah's adoption took over two years and I deemed it our "longest pregnancy." Will's adoption from Hong Kong turned out to be our shortest time of expecting. We started the process in November of 2006 and in April 2007, we flew to Hong Kong to meet and bring Will home. We were met with many surprises, some pleasant and others challenging.

On the first day, the adoption agency set up everything for us and upon our arrival in Hong Kong, we were met by a case worker who brought us to the YWCA, our lodging for the week. The room was clean but extremely small. We were surprised by how small it was.

On the second day, we were brought to Will's orphanage group home and met his house mom as well as the rest of the home residents. He had lived at Pine Hill his whole life, first in the Big House which housed infants to five-year-old's, and then in one of eight group homes designed the same way. His house was a simple twenty-foot by forty-foot building with bunkbed style rooms for four boys and another for four girls with bathrooms for each and a shower in between. There was also a living area, bathroom, and bedroom for the house mom. The ages of the children varied between six and seventeen years old. In addition, there was a kitchen and a common living area. The home was crowded but very neat and tidy. The kids were welcoming and happy. One girl kept tugging at my pants to get my attention. I asked the case worker what she was saying to me. The caseworker wanted me to ignore the girl, but the girl was persistent. So, I asked again. "What is she saying to me?"

"She wants to know if you would take her home also," the caseworker told me reluctantly. How do you shake your head 'no' and comfort a child such as this? It broke my heart. I cried right there in Will's orphanage and I'm crying as I remember and write this experience down.

When we left, we took Will with us. He had said his goodbyes and his orphanage home was no longer his. We did not expect to take Will back to the hotel with us on the second day after we met him, thinking it would be day four or five when we would bring him back with us. It caught us off guard and we even argued that our room did not have a bed for him. "That is not a problem," they said, and ordered a cot to set up at the foot of our bed. The group home mother had packed his bag—a pink Hello Kitty bag—and he was all ours.

Bathing Will that first night was a baptism by fire. He was agitated and kept spitting out the word "Bettina!" in an aggressive fashion, as if he was swearing at us. Finally, Phyllis got in his face with her finger and sternly told him to stop it. It was not how we wanted his first night with us to go, not by a long shot. Later, I asked our caseworker and others who could speak English what Will was saying. No one recognized that word, and to this day it is a mystery.

After showering ourselves we crashed into our bed after a long day. Will fell asleep quickly in his cot, and after hearing his breathing slow, Phyllis leaned into me. "Dirk, what did we do?" she whispered. "What did we do?"

For Phyllis, this was an expression of honest emotion. Besides just being overwhelmed by Will's behavior in the tub, she wasn't feeling well, overall. She has terrible allergies, and in Hong Kong in mid-April, her allergies flared up amid all the springtime blooming.

I believe the Holy Spirit spoke through me in that honest moment.

"We got this Phyllis," I said to her. "With God on our side, we've got this." After a prayer while holding hands we to slipped into a deep sleep.

***

On the third day, we visited Will's school and were able to see him interact with his teachers and friends. The goodbyes at school were tough on him. I think the reality of what was happening began to sink in. This was the first time we saw Will cry. Every time he broke down, tears would fill my eyes too. I have always been the emotional one in our family and still am today. The family can always count on a good cry of happiness or sadness from me at our family get togethers. Thankfully, the caseworkers were there helping us console and encourage him. We spent time in Hong Kong parks during our free time. This was tough on Phyllis because of her allergies, but as always, she was a tough lady and endured. Will and I had fun and enjoyed the weather and the beautiful parks.

On the fourth day, we went out for lunch with Will's "volunteer family." This arrangement puzzled me. Most weekends his volunteer family would pick Will up and have him as a guest in their home. They had two younger sons. Will was attached to and obviously loved them. We went to a Dim Sum restaurant with our caseworker and the volunteer family including grandparents. The restaurant must have been a regular for this family because Will seemed familiar and comfortable with the process. At a Dim Sum restaurant, the waiters and waitresses push carts of various fully prepared foods by your table so the diners can select which foods they want to eat. Since it was Will's last time with the volunteer family, he could pick whatever he wanted for lunch.

He really enjoyed that! The family knew some English and did a good job using it to the best of their ability. With the caseworker translating, the conversation was very cordial and pleasant. Until it wasn't. At one point the grandfather (who did not know English) asked me a question via the caseworker. He had been told I owned ten acres surrounding my home.

"What do you do with your land?" he asked.

I answered that I raised trees to sell to my landscape customers.

The grandfather asked why we were adopting Will. When I explained our intentions were to give Will a loving home and help him be his best, he blew me away with his response.

"Are you adopting Will so he can help you on the farm?"

In other words, were we adopting Will so he could do manual labor for us? I was offended and caught off guard as I stared at his face with its questioning and judgmental demeanor. The social worker was not happy with his line of questioning. But before she could jump in and try and defuse the situation, I blurted out a defense. "That was never even a thought!" I stammered. Thankfully, the caseworker changed the subject and we moved on. I walked away from that lunch conflicted and puzzled. This family obviously loved Will very much. The grandfather even thought we might have nefarious plans for this little boy he and his family had embraced. Why didn't they adopt him? For reasons I will never know.

***

On the fifth day, we were given free entry to Ocean Park, which is a large amusement park. It even has a McDonalds! There was no caseworker along for the ride; it was just the three of us. This proved to be an interesting day as well. Will shied away from the roller coasters and big rides. He liked the children's rides and games. We spent the day riding these rides and playing the games that Will enjoyed. We went for lunch at McDonalds, waiting in line a long time to order and get our food.

What made the day interesting was people's reaction to Will, Phyllis, and me. Our fellow amusement park visitors could not stop staring at us! I guess they could not figure out what this white couple was doing with this Down Syndrome Chinese boy.

When we sat down to eat our food, the passersby would stare so intently they would be several feet past us before turning their heads back to see where they were going. All this craning of necks caused us to look at each other with a smirk. "Take a picture," we joked to each other. "It will last longer!"

Our final day in Hong Day placed us at the offices of local government officials who would approve the adoption process. Our caseworker was there, and we signed off on Will's release along with the adoption agency and government. They were very formal but kind. They thanked us for adopting Will and bringing him to America. The official commended us for our compassionate hearts and financial support of Will. We received Will's paperwork and passport. The final thing was a gift from the people of Hong Kong. I do not remember what it was, but it made us feel appreciated for adopting Will. A feeling I was not expecting but welcomed.

Finally, on Day 7, we were brought to the airport in Hong Kong for our flight home. This would be an eighteen-hour journey back in time so we would land in Grand Rapids, Michigan on the same date. A kind flight attendant in Hong Kong approached us and asked if there was anything we would like her to tell Will in Cantonese.

"It would be great if you explained to Will that the journey is going to be very long," I said. "It would be good if he is patient and if he must go to the toilet to let me know and we will help him." She spoke with him quietly and I could tell he was understanding her. When she was finished, he nodded that he understood, and we were off. Will was a perfect gentleman the entire trip. We could tell his housemothers did a good job teaching him how to be polite and kind.

We landed in early evening to be greeted by our four children and their families. Our grandsons Zach and Corbin were preschool age, and Will had already "met" them via a family video we had made for Bethany. He ran right down the ramp at the airport and gave both those boys huge bear hugs. He even lifted Corbin up off his feet. This was their introduction to Uncle Will, and he to his nephews, a relationship that continues to flourish to this day. Will was so excited to meet his nephews, and Phyllis and I were just as excited to sleep in our own bed with our son asleep down the hall in his.

CHAPTER 4

Challenges in Early Days

Adoption is not for the faint of heart. It is a decision and commitment just like marriage. Our first adoption was motivated by our desire to have a little girl, and the second was driven by God opening our hearts and souls to an older child with significant challenges. The first months in any adoption are hard work— Phyllis and I knew that from adopting before. What we were not prepared for was Will's disability mixed with his language barrier. We experienced plenty of frustrating moments that challenged all three of us.

When we adopted him, Will was nine years old and had been pulled from an environment he was used to, a group home in Hong Kong. His adjustment to our family took a lot of time. He was going through life with no speech and has speech issues to this day. Our son also had some serious attachment issues. Will pulled away from us many times, wanting to be part of his brother's family and not ours. His brother's wife is half Korean, so he may have felt like he wanted to belong to someone who looked like him. He had formulated the ideal living situation for him and we were not the ideal family. During those months Will was convinced he belonged in Dirk III and Tricia's home. They lived close by, and their family was young; his nephews were fun to play with. It was a battle until we made it clear that living with them was not an option. He mourned that realization but eventually accepted it. This resistance to Phyllis and me as his parents was painful, especially for Phyllis. It lead to some intense and teary conversations.

"You are my son, you will live in my home," she would tell a stubborn Will. And then he would go to his "dark space" where his eyes would go hard and flat. He went to this head space when he did not know how to express himself or became frustrated or angry. His eyes became tiny slits and he looked demon possessed. More than once, I commanded the demon out of him in the name of Jesus! Once (and only once) he pounded my chest with his fists out of sheer frustration. I did not know how to react other than to grab him and hold him close until he settled down. Then the tears flowed, and we both wept. Thank goodness, that's hardly a space we ever see him enter anymore. At some point, he accepted that we were his mom and dad and he belonged to us.

Looking back, we do understand his resistance to us and to his new home, country and culture. Will was ingrained in his routine, and we pulled him out of it. This is a guy who *loves* his routine. He prefers to have his day set out for him in an orderly, predictable fashion and to yank him out like that must have been traumatic. When we picked him up in Hong Kong and brought him home to the U.S., he missed his routine, culture and food and being around people who looked like him. He was very sad when he realized it would be his last day at school, too.

Will faced many losses when he was adopted, but he gained a forever family who would do anything to see him thrive and flourish. He was our son from the time we committed to adopt him, even before the first night we were in Hong Kong, and he slept with us in our hotel room. God knew he was our son before that. We were committed to him for the rest of his life. His returning that love and commitment wasn't overnight. Sometimes we wondered if he would ever love us back, but he did. Our faith was rewarded with love.

Slowly but surely our household settled into a routine that worked for all of us. Will loved his social network outside our house. He started school in a CI (cognitively impaired) classroom and did quite well understanding and communicating in class. He was nonverbal but was able to connect. His teachers and friends love him to this day.

Will and I got involved with Special Olympics track and field, bowling and baseball. We joined a Baseball Challengers league where all the players have physical and or cognitive disabilities. Will is very well-coordinated physically and was and is able to do a lot of things other individuals with Down Syndrome would struggle with. One day in our campground, Will and his nephew came riding up on bicycles. We never knew Will could ride a bicycle! Many individuals with Down Syndrome do not have that sense of balance.

Speaking of his nephews, Will now has a total of twelve nieces and nephews. He will sit by any of them that wants a little Uncle Will time, including Brode, who, at seventeen, is disabled and loves one on one time. At a pool party or whatever family event we are at, our son will often go and sit with Brode the whole time.

When Will sees his brothers, they will pull him in for a man hug. He is like the cool man on campus with his fist bumps. They are all good to him and encourage him every time they see him. Even though we struggled at first, it's now hard to imagine Will being in any other family but ours.

Currently, Will has two years left in his school transitions program and then it will be time for him to move into a job in our community. If you ask him what he wants to do when he is done with school his response is "deli." A job at a grocery store deli would be great thing for him. And when you ask him where he wants to live, he says "with Mom and Dad." We've come a long way.

CHAPTER 5

A Shred Catches Fire

During the summer of 2016 I took Will with me to work to give his mother a break. By this time, he was twenty years old, and he looked forward to something to do during his summer vacation. I had many boxes of old documents that needed to be shredded. Will would set up his station with music coming from an external speaker or using ear buds. He liked the consistency and the lunches his mom packed. He wore out a shredder in the month, so I bought him a better machine. At the end of each week, we took the shredded paper to a paper gator (a recycling initiative). Soon he ran out of documents to shred, so I started to appeal to neighbors, family, and friends. Along with that plea and social media marketing, he always had enough shredding work to keep him busy. (His mother was overjoyed to have Will doing work he was capable of and genuinely enjoyed.)

Having Will come to work with me and shred paper sparked a tiny idea in me that would eventually ignite into my passion project— Beyond26. But I'll get to that in a minute.

A friend seriously fueled the flames of this tiny spark. In 2017, Bob Wondergem, the coordinator of the Challengers Baseball League and I began talking about the prospect of our sons eventually aging out of the school system at age twenty-six. We wondered out loud what would be available for them in the job market and how could we advocate for them.

At the time, the conversations focused on Bob's son who was older than Will and closer to aging out. My friend said how tough it would be to find a job for individuals like his son, who like Will is cognitively impaired. He could read, however, and we both knew there was something productive he could be doing when he aged out of the school system. We agreed there was a need in the community for a nonprofit which focused on finding employment for individuals with disabilities. Bob was passionate about finding employment for people such as his son and others. (He eventually became our board president and has been an essential figure in our journey.)

At that point, his son was in the program Will is in currently: the Transitions program through Kent ISD (Intermediate School District). From their website:

"All students leave school to create their adult lives. "Transition" describes that critical transformation and includes the education, legal information, planning, and community connections our special education students need to achieve adult goals. The transition process prepares students with disabilities for adult life by focusing on the specific areas of post-secondary education, employment, community participation, and when appropriate, independent living skills."

Part of Will's days at his Transitions program is volunteering at businesses that let him and his cohorts come in and work with them. One such business work site is Beer City Dog Biscuits, a nonprofit business set up for two young men on the autism spectrum by their mothers. They get leftover beer mash from Founders Brewing Company in Grand Rapids and turn it into nutritious dog biscuits.

Their core mission, "to empower the disabled through the creation of our dog biscuits," underscores everything they do. "A vibrant living community for those with development disabilities is the long-term vision of this nonprofit," their website states. "The immediate need is to provide them with an opportunity to be productive every day."

Being productive means that their "Brew Bakers," a team of disabled adults, develop skills through each step of the biscuit baking process, from mixing dough to packaging biscuits. 100% of donations and sales are re-invested into their mission to support disabled adults in their personal and professional growth.

The Brew Bakers' daily tasks are tailored to meet the unique abilities of each volunteer and employee. These employees must be independently mobile with relatively good fine motor skills and be able to follow simple 1-2 step directions. Some employees plan and forecast demand or identify sales opportunities, calculating costs or counting cash and credit sales. Others mix dough, which includes following a recipe, or stuff biscuit molds, which hones their fine motor skills. Yet others stuff and weigh bags, which help them practice their quantitative measuring skills; operate the machinery that seals and labels bags, or maybe assist in dishwashing and kitchen cleanup. Every task teaches valuable life skills and builds community as the employees stand shoulder to shoulder, day by day.

***

Businesses such as Beer City Dog Biscuits are an inspiring example of what can happen when the community surrounds and supports its disabled young adults. This is what every parent of a disabled child wants for them—to earn the dignity that comes from being productive in whatever form that takes. When Will started coming to work with me, he joined his siblings at the building we all share for our various businesses. Leah works for her brothers Dirk III and Kyle who now own the businesses I started. Josh is a partner of a dumpster rental company and manages the day-to-day operations. To have Will there working alongside us all is meaningful. His siblings are in and out of the workspace, always ready to offer a fist bump and a "Good job, keep it up, Bud." Life is good as Will gets positive reinforcement from his family.

When he started off, Will was in an area by himself. He would get into the zone with a box of paper in front of him, listening to Taylor Swift or Selena Gomez (or sometimes the Chipmunks) on his Beats headphones. He's really into music.

Will quickly learned how to shred paper and fell into a good routine at work. Sometimes he would have to be reminded to take a lunch break, and then that break would extend itself—just a little bit. Will can take a lunch and turn it into an hour and a half experience. Each day he takes his dollar bill and goes to the vending machine in the back and buys himself a Coke.

It's a friendly routine, a good routine, one that would one day come to expand and include more community members, eight to twelve job seekers who join my family at the building every day from Monday to Thursday, shredding paper and building dignity. It all started with a spark of an idea when Phyllis and I wanted to get Will out of the house in the summertime. But then again, I am getting ahead of myself a little bit. The idea for Beyond 26 was going to germinate for a while before taking root.

CHAPTER 6

Beginnings and Beyond

One conversation with Bob turned into more conversations which led to a monthly round table discussions at a local restaurant. We slowly began inviting other like-minded individuals who either were connected somehow through family to young adults with disabilities or worked in the disability community. Soon we had a retired schoolteacher who spent her career in special education, my niece who is a lawyer, my sister who is a gifted administrator and a CPA who specializes in nonprofit accounting. We were off to a strong start.

Our group understood that twenty-six is a critical age for an adult with disabilities; this is the age of discovery and the year they age out of Michigan's education system. While the next step should likely be employment, these opportunities were, unfortunately, few and far between for adults with disabilities. We aimed to bridge this gap between local businesses and a community of jobseekers through employment and volunteer opportunities.

My first volunteer and now board member was Ellie Van Keulen, a retired teacher who worked with individuals with disabilities. She recognized that many of her former students were sitting at home doing nothing. Ellie started meeting with our round table during the early months. She had kept in touch with some of her old students and contacted them. That group of former students became our first jobseekers. Ellie initially did all our Meet and Greet sessions, which are a simple but vital part of our program. The purpose of the Meet & Greet (M&G) is to listen to the hopes and dreams of the jobseeker while determining potential job sites based on their skills, necessary accommodations, and personality. Here's how it works: Ellie, another intake specialist or I reach out to the jobseeker to get basic details such as contact information, and sets up an appointment for an M&G.

The intake specialist makes sure that the jobseeker understands that this is not an interview, but a get-to-know-you-session. Next, the intake specialist will distribute a question guide to the jobseeker and walk through it while taking notes of the jobseeker's responses. This is a straightforward discussion with the jobseeker about how long they are willing to wait for employment, whether they need to be paid or receive a certain number of hours and how flexible they are with compromising certain aspects of their job search.

It's key to respectfully pay attention to the dreams and goals of each jobseeker. It can feel like a stretch to keep jobseeker dreams in mind and be realistic at the same time, but dreams matter. For example, we had a jobseeker who dreamed of being a voice actor. Since he did not need a paid position, he began his own podcast with our help, and had it published by a local news company. Another jobseeker whose goal was to work with flowers *did* need paid work, so she got a job at a local grocery store with a large garden center.

After the Meet and Greet, the search for employment or volunteer opportunities begins! (You can read more in our program guide at the back of this book.) Slowly, Ellie and our team refined our systems and processes into what they are today.

Before we could match jobseekers with jobs, I had to know that we were filling a real need in the community. I began to ask anyone and everyone, is there a need? I asked that question repeatedly, in the community, among business leaders, among parents of young adults with disabilities. I kept knocking on doors and I kept getting the affirmations I was seeking: It was a resounding yes! So many individuals fall between the cracks and end up sitting at home with no work or social community. There was a need for an organization like the one I was dreaming about with my fellow visionaries with a heart for young adults with disabilities. Beyond26, as the Board and I had decided to name it, was and is needed in West Michigan. West Michigan, yes, and beyond. The main reason for this need was and is because of our laser focus on employment. Our model is focused on jobs like a horse with blinders on.

Other local agencies that work with individuals with disabilities have some of the other services covered. You can send your adult dependent child to a job readiness program. They can receive transportation and health care. Some agencies also help their individuals with disabilities find jobs, but it is not their focus. Jobs are our focus!

I spent most of the year speaking to anyone that would listen. I met with Disability Advocates of Kent County, Network 180, Hope Network, Goodwill, IKUS, Special Olympics, ARC, MRS and any other agency that services individuals with disabilities. I had so much to learn, but I knew there was a need to fill, and that need was jobs.

In January of 2018, we submitted for a 501c3 nonprofit status from the IRS. We had already submitted necessary forms to operate as a business in the USA and the State of Michigan. In March 2018 we received our 501c3 approval. The name of the newly organized nonprofit was Beyond26 Inc, a name that symbolizes that age when our jobseekers age out of the school system in the State of Michigan. The Board of Directors asked me to lead the company as the Executive Director. Since it was so new, I knew I had my work cut out for me. Beyond26 became my passion project. The young upstart had no social media presence, no jobseeker clients, no website, and no financial backing. But that would soon change.

***

My second volunteer was my friend Denny. He had recently retired and had an interest in helping us launch Beyond26. He assumed the role of Job Developer in early 2019 and found many of the business partners that still offer employment to our jobseekers today. Denny's style was to stop in and meet potential business partners, leave a card and brochure, and move on. His success rate was impressive, and he was able to get some strong businesses involved in our work, including Panera Bread, Grist Mill, J&H Family Stores, Meijer, and Tech Defenders.

At times he would have a dozen jobseekers needing jobs. He had the patience to work with them one at a time to match them with the best possible jobs. Denny gave us a year of his talent until we had the financial budget to hire a job developer. I will always be grateful for Denny, Ellie, and the other early believers in the vision to match jobseekers with jobs.

***

By the end of 2018, Beyond26 we received a sizable donation from a Charitable Trust.

One of my contacts worked at an employment agency. She would occasionally send me a referral to a company that has a heart for employing individuals with disabilities. One of those referrals turned into something more. I was just starting my presentation to the HR team member when she stopped me and said her CEO wanted to know more about Beyond26. He joined us in her office, and I introduced Beyond26 the same way I have been telling others our story. My job as Executive Director is to fill 4 pipelines: Jobseekers, Business Partners, Volunteers and Donors.

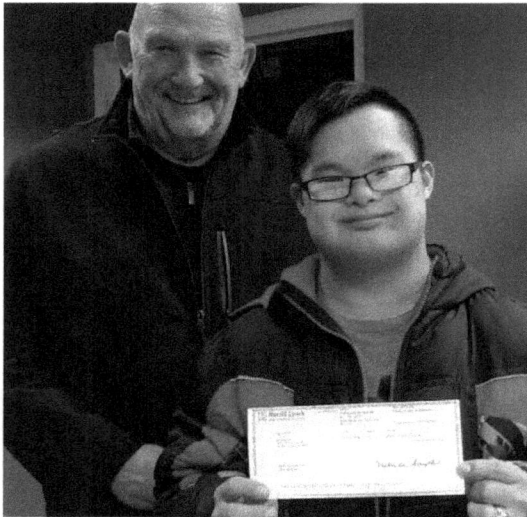

"If there are any one of those pipelines you could help with, I would be appreciative," I said. They thanked me for coming and said they would get back to me. About a month later I received an email from the CEO. He asked me to put together a proforma he could present to his Board of Directors for the charitable trust he helps administer. I did my best but thought my proforma effort was crude. He thanked me and in November 2018, a $31,000 check came in the mail! This was the single largest gift given to Beyond26 at that time. This charitable trust continues to support us on an annual basis. We are so thankful for that referral, but mostly to God, who leads us exactly where we should go.

***

Our first jobseeker was Dahlia, a young lady with autism. She had a delightful personality but a rather rigid set of goals. She wanted to work with dogs, and she wanted to be paid. We built a profile on her past experiences and schooling, including her current contact information as well as a picture. The third column in the profile we built was designated for supports she would need to be successful in a job. Dahlia really wanted a job in a big national chain pet store,

26

so we researched it. There were no available jobs for her there, so she waited, and we waited for the right opportunity to surface. Finally, a dog kennel was willing to give her a job on a trial basis. The manager seemed very willing to work with her and agreed that her Community Living Supports (CLS) worker could be there on her first day to coach and encourage. (CLS services are meant to provide skills training and personal assistance to help increase an individual with disabilities' level of independence in their home and their community.)

When Dahlia came to work on her first day, the manager that hired her was not there and the person in charge would not allow her CLS worker/coach to help her in the kennel area because company policy did not allow it. Dahlia did not appreciate the job she was given—cleaning kennels—because in her mind she thought she would be playing with and exercising dogs. So, her first day was her last day. Epic fail! This was hard to process on all fronts. A year later she was offered a volunteer position at a dog training business. This too was a failure because she wanted to be paid and the dogs were too large. Her mom graciously realized that her daughter would likely never get a paid job playing with dogs, so she asked me to take her off the jobseeker list.

From this difficult first experience, I learned something valuable: There will be some people who come to us whom we won't be able to serve. This young lady was one of them. Dahlia had a one-track mind. She wanted to do one thing. The concept of starting at the bottom, doing menial work, and paying your dues wasn't acceptable to her. She wanted to be paid to play with dogs and she didn't have the flexibility to imagine doing other work involving dogs.

Fortunately, failures like this are the exception and not the rule. Our stated mission, "Find Jobs & Volunteer Opportunities for Individuals with Disabilities," was being realized. Our goal, "to bridge the gap between local businesses and a community of jobseekers by using positive engagement through employment and volunteer opportunities" was being reached. In our first year we were able to place thirty-five jobseekers in jobs or volunteer opportunities that fit their profile and within their own community. Unlike Dahlia, most of our jobseekers *do* have the flexibility that is often required of an employee. I have found that if these individuals are doing something they like and they like the people they are working with, they will be content to do that job for the rest of their lives.

CHAPTER 7

The Power of Paper Shredding

As time has gone on, I have come to know a lot of people in the disability world, and I've come to know our job seekers, some of them very well. They have a unique ability to see people exactly where they are at in life with no judgment. In addition, they are honest and true to who they are, no pretenses. The beautiful thing is that I don't have pretenses around them either—what a relief!

One example of a no-pretense guy is Riley, who worked in our paper shredding microbusiness: Beyond26 Document Shredding (more on that in a moment). What you see is what you get with Riley. He puts in a good day of work "paper shredding." "I help put it through the machine," he says. "We put it in a box where they take it a place where they make new paper out of it. I love that, saving the earth."

Obviously, Riley has a very green sensibility, and the earth-friendly business of shredding paper to be made into new paper is of value to him. But that's not his favorite part of the job. If you ask him what that is, he has a quick answer. "Teasing Dirk," he will say. "He's my man."

Riley has moved on from our Document Shredding program to a job in his community, but before he left, he wanted to let everyone know, "If you need a job, ask Dirk. He's my man. He will help you if you need the help."

Today we have eight to thirteen job seekers who work Monday through Thursday at our document shredding facility, but it all started with Will.

Along with my board of directors, we decided the document shredding that Will was doing during the summer months would be a micro business we could use to test our jobseekers' abilities, and a training center to find their potential. Once the jobseekers spent time working here, we could analyze if they had the capacity to work a different job. We began operating Monday-Thursday from 9 a.m. to 2 p.m., with thirteen jobseekers and three part time supervisors. Some of the jobseekers work short shifts and others work multiple days. The supervisors are paid, and the jobseekers are volunteers that receive a once-a-month stiped based on how much time they work in their volunteer positions. One month we might give them a gift card, and the next month a little cash. They are always thrilled on payday. It means the world to them to get paid.

Pete is one of our jobseekers at the document shredding business. He and his family live on a working farm. Pete has cognitive disabilities and in addition suffers from occasional seizures which over time has affected his balance. His mom drives him to Beyond26 Document Shredding every Tuesday to work for the day. This affords her a respite time to do those things that cannot get done otherwise. It is time she needs and deserves. Pete can do a job that he is good at. He gets to talk to others and share his deepest wish (which is that he has no more seizures). Pete loves to tease me and ask for a raise (I love this about him). He is at home and is comfortable in his work community. This is what a work community creates for an individual with a disability. A safe place to be.

Our customers bring us old files they no longer need, such as old customer files, financial and tax files, old work orders, estimates and other documents they don't need to keep on hand anymore.

One regular customer uses a large quantity of engineered designs for printing cardboard box logos, and we pick up two or three tubs of documents from them every week. There are many services for hire to shred paper: Shred it, Rapid Shred, West Michigan Document Shredding, and the list goes on. They will typically come to your place of business once a month or whatever. They can shred them on site at your place of business or back at their place of business. We suggest a donation of $10 a box to shred a businesses or individual's paper, which is a competitive rate. What we offer our customers, though, goes beyond a simple

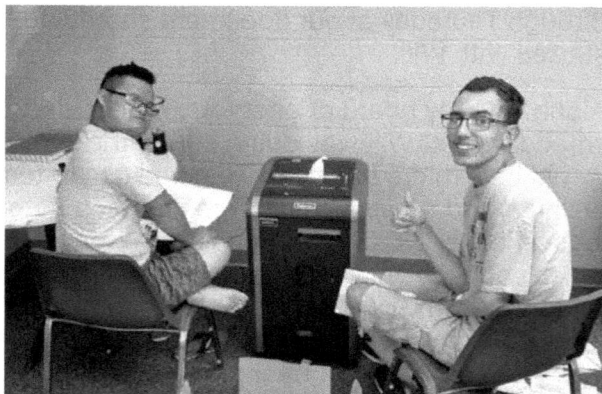

transaction.

From our website: "Document Shredding assists individuals with disabilities by providing volunteer opportunities to develop job readiness skills. Our team is passionate about shredding documents. They are always eager to work and in constant need of more paper to shred. Because of that, Beyond26 is more than happy to take care of your document shredding needs. With your help, we can keep this program alive and well."

At the start, we advertised through word of mouth and social media and began to get plenty of referrals. This was a need in the business community that could be filled by our jobseekers, who benefit from the dignity and value of work and the much-needed routine and the community that is built on the job. Today Beyond26 Document Shredding is self-sustaining as far as paper goes. We used to run out of documents and would shut down operations from time to time. Now we have enough traction and customers to keep everyone busy. In fact, we are planning a second location and new document shredding facility in Grand Haven, Michigan, to keep up with demand. People there are on fire about this program and our model, and it's exciting to expand.

***

We couldn't run this enterprise without our volunteers, one of whom is Herb, who works one morning shift per week driving around and picking up boxes for us from various customers. On his morning at Beyond26 document shredding, Herb jumps in the delivery van, armed with his list and a two-wheel dolly, and roams around the region picking up paper for us to shred. We used to have a jobseeker who liked to go with him, but Herb doesn't mind doing it on his own. Sometimes there will be a one-off pickup, such as a school calling and saying they have, say, fourteen boxes of paper for us to shred.

Andrea is a document shredding supervisor who is also the administrative supervisor. A few of her hours are used for fielding calls and email requests. She also schedules the jobseekers, finds substitutes for supervisor time off, sets up the monthly pickup route and schedules one-time pick-up requests. She and I usually make decisions together to close for snow days or other types of unforeseen circumstances. It's a blessing to have a supervisor to take care of the day-to-day operations, freeing me up for other parts of my role.

Though successful in many ways, the document shredding wing of Beyond26 still requires fund raising. Even though the jobseekers are volunteers, and we ask for a suggested donation of $10 per bankers' box, we do pay our supervisors and do not take in enough revenue to sustain this department. Thankfully, our donors are faithful and this revenue can be included in our programming budget.

When I look back at what was set in motion when Phyllis and I strived to give Will something to do in the summers, I can hardly believe it. Little did I know this would turn into something much bigger.

So far, we have graduated three jobseekers, including Riley, who moved into paid positions in the community. This was always our goal, to assess these jobseekers, train them in job skills and move them into their communities and paid employment. It's wonderful when we can have reunion pizza lunches with our "alumni." The jobseekers past and present are delighted to see each other again.

One beautiful benefit for me has been to see to how positively the jobseekers affect the whole work culture at the building where we house our four family companies. The staff are so gracious to the Beyond 26 team, interacting with them daily as they walk through the facility with their bags of shredded documents. My son Josh can see the Go Bus (the minibus that transports people with disabilities) from his office window, and he has designated himself as the person who watches for the bus and alerts the jobseekers that it has arrived to carry them home. The other day he texted me with a photo of my personal Beyond26 coffee mug. "Do you have one of these for your Go Bus spotter?" he asked. I think that's a reasonable request, considering his services to the team.

One of our jobseekers, Mike, loves to wander around the building and especially enjoys talking to my daughter, Leah. She is the popcorn maker-in-chief around the company, so that may be part of the reason she's so popular. Mike will wander into her office, which is conveniently located by the popcorn machine. "Makin' popcorn today?" Mike will ask. Leah doesn't mind popping a batch to put a smile on Mike's face. "I guess I better do that now," she will say. It's all in a day's work in the Beyond26 world. He makes her day, and she makes his.

***

For me to give back in this way, at age sixty-six, is inspiring and fuels my passion. This is where God has placed me for right now.

Beyond26 is a faith-based nonprofit; it's faith that motivates us. One of our core values is showing the love and care of Jesus Christ. Our website says, "We aim to demonstrate the love and support of Jesus Christ as we work with individuals before, during and after the employment process."

Our board is made up of ten individuals who either have a child with a disability or have a connection through their work or family. We come from different faith practices with one unified stand: that we serve our jobseekers. We never impose our faith practices on others, we only serve by living our faith. We also do not charge a fee for the service to either the jobseeker or our business partners. This is the best, most uncomplicated practice. People can come to us knowing we will be their advocate and their child's advocate from the beginning of the process to completion. This is a commitment we embrace for life. Jobseekers are welcome to come back to us a second or third time because the first job did not work out. Much like us, they have failures, and we stand ready to serve them as they find their footing again.

Since we seek to include individuals with disabilities into

our communities through employment, we also are inclusive regarding race and alternative lifestyles. We need to show our faith to all people without judgment. Our jobseekers' model this for us. They love the people around them without preconceived judgements. "Love everybody" is the theme. In many senses they are God's perfect, loving society. A great example for all of us.

CHAPTER 8

Success Stories, Part One

Jeff is the son of two of our board members Bob and Vicki Wondergem. He aged out of the school system at age twenty-six, several years ago. Now he attends programming through Hope Network three days a week, and shreds paper for us at Beyond26 Document Shredding on Mondays. These daily outings provide him with a social network and a community. Jeff is a stickler for time and uses his time efficiently. The other day I noticed that his Go Bus was waiting outside for him a bit early at the end of the day.

"Hey, Jeff, your Go Bus is outside," I told him.

"He can wait," Jeff said, taking his sweet time and not stopping what he was doing. "He's early!"

Before Covid, Jeff, working alongside his job coach, also volunteered one morning per week at the Community Food Club in an underserved area of Grand Rapids.

The Community Food Club is a non-profit, member-based grocery store. Low-income members pay between $11 and $15 for a 30-day membership and can shop using points based on their household size. Most members receive nine to eleven days' worth of food during each membership period. Members can shop as often as they'd like and select foods that fit their needs.

From their website: "Traditional grocery store pricing is turned upside down at the Community Food Club – fruits and vegetables are the lowest priced items while processed foods and snack items are among the highest priced. This incentivizes healthy options and increases access to fresh, nutritious foods on a consistent basis. At the Food Club, we are committed to always stocking fresh fruits, vegetables, meat, cheese, milk, and eggs. Fruits and vegetables make up 42% of the item's members select – nearly triple the average amount distributed by traditional grocery stores."

Jeff worked as a stocking volunteer. He stocked, organized and straightened products on the store shelves and in their coolers. For Jeff, this time was a giveback for him, a time to do something extra to contribute to the community and enhance the lives of community members.

Jeff's week is uniquely full for a young adult with disabilities. His work is unpaid, although he does receive a small stipend for his work at Beyond26 Document Shredding. Believe me, he is on top of that money gift! He will be sure and let me know in clear terms if I have gotten behind on my payroll.

Alice is cognitively impaired and legally blind. She has recently started volunteering at Potter Park Zoo in Lansing, Michigan, a 20-acre zoo within an 80-acre park featuring over 500 animal residents. She and her mom have been proactive in getting a volunteer job in the community. Nick, our job developer, researched the zoo job and introduced it to them. Because of her impairments, this placement is a victory. Her job at the zoo? Making Christmas ornaments for the zoo trees!

Jillian was a job seeker on our books for about nine months. Her disability is more emotional than cognitive. She is very smart, but socially lacks the capacity to function in a normal working environment because of her high anxiety. Finding a job for her was tough. We couldn't find anything that fit her profile.

I decided to drive to her house and interview her and her mom. This visit was much like a second meet and greet. On my way home, I decided to research businesses around her house, thinking she would be more comfortable in a familiar environment. Because Jillian requires a service animal to help her cope, I thought the vet nearby her house might be a good fit. The vet was sympathetic but pointed out that her service animal would likely agitate his furry patients. So that was out. But he did suggest I check in at the flower shop next door to his vet practice.

May, the owner of the flower shop, is a one woman show who

mostly does weddings. She was open to the idea of Jillian coming in and had no issue with her bringing her service dog. They would both be welcome and May needed extra help on Tuesday afternoons after the weekly delivery of flowers from vendors.

"I need someone to help process the flowers to be used in bouquets," she said. Jillian is still actively involved there and now has the confidence to drive herself and her dog to work! This very part time job has been instrumental in bringing Jillian out of her shell. Jillian's mom still thanks me all the time for going the extra mile in finding a good fit for her daughter. May, the owner of the flower shop, had this to say about Jillian: "She is a big help! She does many of the tasks I struggle to get done. She is very flexible as well. I appreciate her help very much."

Andy is still in school in the Transitions program, but he spends one afternoon a week at Panera Bread, where he enjoys bussing tables and serving meals to hungry diners. Early on in our program, our volunteer Denny connected with Bonnie, the manager of a Panera Bread branch near Andy's house. He told her about Andy and our mission: to provide dignity and purpose via jobs for young adults with disabilities. Andy's parents didn't want Andy to be paid for his work, lest it interfere with his other government benefits, but they along with their son wanted to find a volunteer position for him. Bonnie graciously allowed Andy to come in as a volunteer, which he loved, that is until Covid hit. Every time I would see him for a year and a half he would always say, "I want to go back to Panera Bread." He loved interacting with people on his afternoons there.

When it became safe and possible for Andy to return, Bonnie had left the restaurant, which was now managed by someone else. When Andy's mother approached the new manager about bringing Andy back on, the answer was no. They didn't have any volunteers, only paid employees. Andy's mom was disappointed, but she asked where Bonnie had gone to. When she was told that Bonnie was managing a different Panera Bread restaurant, not too far away, she found Bonnie and −you guessed it—Andy is back as a volunteer at his favorite place, though a slightly different location, bussing tables and serving meals to customers. "At my new job, I've learned how to be careful to make sure my workspace is neat," says Andy. "It's helped me be more helpful at home too. I'm proud of a job well done." This story illustrates the truth that you must keep trying until you talk to the right person.

Andy's parents didn't want him to have paid employment, a mindset shared by many parents of young adults with disabilities. These parents are concerned that their child will lose part of their Social Security Disability benefits. Depending on the income, they may lose some benefits, but not their Medicaid. Basically, if they work fifteen hours or less per week, they won't lose any benefits, but many parents are still afraid of reporting their child's work. They would rather just avoid the whole issue and have their child volunteer.

However, many young adults with disabilities want to be paid for their work and their parents support them all the way.

Sarah is one such young adult who also works for Panera Bread as a paid employee. Recently, she was named Employee of the Month, and she has proudly chosen the commemorative photo of her and her manager as her Facebook profile picture. Just like all our jobseekers, Sarah's job means everything to her.

CHAPTER 9

Lessons Learned the Hard Way

Not every story has a happy ending, or in our case, a smooth path to success and a good match between jobseeker and job. Some of our jobseekers are working in their community within days, others need to wait months for the right opportunity.

You always learn something from your failures, probably more than you ever would from your successes, though your failures feel bad, and your successes feel good. I learned something big from my biggest failure so far at Beyond26.

We had a young jobseeker—I will call him Austin—who wanted to get a job stocking shelves at a big store. Austin, who has Asperger's Syndrome, applied for, and got an interview at Farm & Fleet. His mom asked if I would be willing to accompany him at the interview, and of course I said yes. They had experienced many disappointments already with various agencies who had not been able to help Austin get a job.

Things were going well when the people conducting the interview began talking about a maintenance job which involved scrubbing floors and cleaning toilets. Austin seemed to take this in stride and answered affirmatively when he was asked if he would be interested in that kind of a job. "I could do that," he answered. At that point, I jumped in and reiterated that Austin wanted a job stocking shelves. "We don't have any jobs right now stocking shelves, but we do have this one in maintenance available," the interviewer said.

Austin once again repeated that it was okay, he would do the job they were offering him. And they did offer him the job, which he accepted, and they began outlining what next steps were as far as paperwork and getting started at their store.

When we left the store, I gave him a high five. "Congratulations!" I said jubilantly. "You got the job!" But Austin looked anything but jubilant. His face did not look like the face of a guy who just scored a job. He looked devastated.

His mom met us in the parking lot and could see immediately that something was wrong. "What happened?" Austin fell into her arms and began to bawl on her shoulder.

I explained that he had gotten a job, but it wasn't one stocking shelves, it was a maintenance position. Whoa—the mom changed her attitude in a flash. She was livid. "You were supposed to advocate for him!" she raged. (Of course, my mild interjection, that I had tried, fell on deaf ears.) "You're just like every other agency out there!" She demanded I take Austin's name out of our database and added that she hoped she would never see me again. It was scorched earth. I couldn't believe it.

Yet, later, when I had the chance to process the experience and reflect, I realized that she had been right. I didn't try hard enough to advocate for Austin and to make it clear that he wanted a job stocking shelves, not scrubbing toilets. I lacked understanding of his disability, and how an experience like this disappointing job interview might cause Austin to react the way he did. He simply did not have the social cues or confidence to speak up for himself and be clear about what kind of job he did and didn't want. I also know that his mom's outsized anger wasn't just directed at me, it was aimed at every disappointing person and experience along the path for her as she tried to help get her son a job.

Lesson learned the hard way: if the job doesn't fit what the jobseeker wants, you might as well shut down the interview right then and there. The job and the jobseeker must be a good match.

***

Our weekly Tuesday meetings are vital to our process. We review the list of jobseekers every team meeting and sometimes more than one of us will gang up on a jobseeker's search to speed up the process. The meeting includes Emily, our Development Director and Communications Specialist, Ellie, Board member volunteer, Nick, our Job Developer, Elisa, our Administrative Assistant, and me. We brainstorm what jobs and employers might be a good fit for a particular jobseeker and we scan and rescan our list of business partners. To boil it down, we shake the tree on a weekly basis.

In keeping our focus like this, we prevent mission drift. "Put on the blinders team," I will often say. "We have a job to do, our jobseekers are our number one priority!"

Our process is simple and does not require a lot of testing or paperwork. Our meet and greet is thorough and once a profile

is developed, we can dive right into the job search process.
Our profile has three columns: One column lists a jobseeker's schooling and work experience. The second column provides a picture of the jobseeker, current contact information, their ideal job (if known), and how many hours per week they want to work. Some want to work for pay and others would like to volunteer. We work with them to find their ideal job. The third column lists the supports that would help the jobseeker be successful in a job. This transparency is critical to our potential employers; there is no hidden agenda.

For many jobseekers, this will be their first job. Our job developer tries to identify any concerns that the jobseeker may have about job readiness. Sometimes this is just a matter of discussing appropriate workplace etiquette such as attendance and dress code policies. For some jobseekers, you may need to get more specific about what parts of a job are a "yes" and what parts are a "no," such as: Are they able to read a list of instructions? Are they able to count money? Are they computer literate? Are they able to lift heavy weights? All these questions will help define job readiness and help the job find the right placement.

Being an employer myself, I know there is nothing worse than interviewing someone and considering a potential employee for your business without knowing the nuances of that employee. It's very important that our Beyond26 employers know that a jobseeker is coming to work in a wheelchair or is easily distracted and prone to wandering. We aim to be as clear as possible, because then they will better know the answers to questions such as "Are you able to accommodate and manage these things at your place of business?" Most often we can ward off future difficulties through this transparent conversation, but not always.

Take the case of two sisters we have been working with, Ashley and Abigail. Both are in their mid-twenties with cognitive disabilities and high levels of anxiety. They are sometimes afraid of being around other people. These sisters have been difficult to place. Because our job developer's case load was getting so full, our board member and ace volunteer, Ellie, decided to take them on herself. She met with the sisters and their mom and was able to initially place Ashley, who was interested in baking, in a bagel shop for early three and a half hour shifts. Ashley's mom got up and drove Ashley to the bagel shop for a four-a.m. start time, so hats off to her for that! She was on time for every shift and really tried to make it work, but in the end, the responsibilities were beyond her capacity. She had problems following specific instructions and no matter how much good coaching she was getting from Ellie and her bosses; she couldn't get past this issue. Her boss let us know after a couple of weeks that the situation wasn't working out. Currently, Ellie is helping Ashley look for another food-related job that requires less responsibility and more routine. We do have some ideas; after all, we have about fifty business partners to scan for a match. The experience wasn't a total wash. Ashley, who was homeschooled and hasn't been around a lot of people before, got a valuable taste of what it would be like to have a job.

Things have also been tough for Abigail, Ashley's sister. Placed at a thrift store connected to a nonprofit, Abigail's duties were to take in donations, helping to sort various household items and clothes and fold clothes. Her hours have been more erratic than the thrift store would like, and they would like to see her increase her speed at folding clothes. We are still waiting to see if she can build up stamina and hang in there with them; the jury is still out. To add to the complexity, neither Ashley nor Abigail have been diagnosed, which means they are not getting any social service support either. We're just going to keep trying until we find a good match for these sisters.

***

Sometimes our job seekers have many qualities that are attractive to employers: stamina, intelligence, and even education. But those things don't always translate to success on the job. Benjamin, for example, is autistic and has a degree in computer sciences. We helped him get an internship with a good company that could have led to a paid position, but it didn't work out. Somewhat related to his disability, Benjamin suffers from frequent insomnia and was too tired to get up in the mornings and make it for the 9 a.m. team meetings. He got Covid 19, as well, which led to him missing more work, so he was let go from his internship. Benjamin would like to have a position working remotely from home, but to request that from the get-go may not be a realistic ask. It will be difficult to place him, as it will be to place Caleb, also autistic, who is a writer and would love to be published. The only problem is, he has no published works, and you need "clips," even in newsletters or other unpaid publications. That's the way the writing world works. While we work on that, we are hopeful we can place Caleb a writing-adjacent job in a library or bookstore, where he would be surrounded with words and books.

***

On rare occasions the workplace itself is inhospitable to a jobseeker, or maybe it's fairer to say a few bad apples are inhospitable. Nolan is one of three jobseekers who we helped place at a large distribution center. This distribution center is noted for its openness to employing and supporting people with disabilities, and Nolan was off to a strong start, even running his own pallet truck, a small forklift designed for moving pallet-sized loads through a warehouse.

But Nolan, who is autistic, was experiencing some difficulties with a couple of his coworkers, who were taking advantage of him. "Hey, can I borrow $10?" they would say, and Nolan, wanting to be liked, would readily give them the cash. Of course, they didn't pay him back. Nolan lives with his grandma, and when she caught wind of this she stepped in and nipped it in the bud, even though Nolan was afraid to speak up. He didn't want the guys to dislike him. Soon after, the situation resolved itself when Nolan wanted to move to a workplace closer to his home.

***

Some of our job seekers need encouragement from a source outside their inner circles. Lisa has a physical disability and is in a wheelchair. She has a degree in education and dreams of being a para pro in the school system. Joe, also in a wheelchair, has cerebral palsy. He is educated and is seeking a job in development at a nonprofit.

You may wonder why folks such as Lisa and Joe need our help in the first place. To be honest, they only need our help in one crucial area: giving them the confidence that yes, they can go out into the world, apply for, and get jobs they can do well. We see this time and time again—jobseekers see themselves as being at a disadvantage, but after they go through our process, they gain that boost they need to move forward with their heads held high. Both these jobseekers are currently interviewing for positions in their fields and are moving full steam ahead.

My second favorite thing is when jobseekers such as Joe and Lisa end up taking the bull by the horns and applying for their own jobs. My first favorite thing? When they get the job, and they did it all on their own.

CHAPTER 10

We Couldn't Do It Without Ellie

Ellie is a mainstay of Beyond26. She volunteers her time up to and beyond thirty hours per week, lending us her expertise and giving of herself to the jobseekers. One by one, our jobseekers have gone through the meet and greet process, and for some of them, it is their former teacher, whom they call Q, who is there for them again as a coach, encourager, and guiding hand.

No book about Beyond26 would be complete without her voice, so consider this: the Ellie Chapter, filled with her wisdom and the stories of jobseekers who have benefitted from her coaching and compassion.

Q and A with "Q"

Q: What is behind your passion for Beyond26?

Ellie: I facilitated inclusion at South Christian High School for twenty-four years. When I retired, I saw my former students sitting at home and not doing anything. This was detrimental to them, and I saw them deteriorate in some ways, physically, mentally and socially. People with Down Syndrome, for example, will gain weight when they are not active, which affects their health risks. Mentally and emotionally, they have lost their circle of friends and their connections. After school, they are no longer included in the social scene. They lose all of that when they sit home. They lose their friends, who go to college, or they have jobs, and they don't get to see them anymore.

I knew my former students and other young adults with disabilities had gifts to give to the community. It became my passion to help them use their gifts through work, which would provide a social context and other important benefits for them.

Kayla, for example, was sitting at home, as a very abled young lady with Down Syndrome. She only had moderate impairments and her daily skill levels tested higher. Her ability to reason and problem solve are amazing, even though she can't read and write very well. Kayla was one of the first people at Beyond26 document shredding, and she's good at it. When I recently asked her if she could take over as the boss, she smiled and said, "Q, of course!"

Q: What does Beyond26's vision of working "shoulder to shoulder" mean to you?"

Ellie: To me, "shoulder to shoulder" means we work together with our jobseekers, their parents, our business partners, and the community to support them and each other. Our jobseekers are contributing and the community is blessed and becomes richer. Businesses can bless jobseekers with work that gives them purpose and dignity. It's a two-way street. Businesses and coworkers need to exhibit a quality of respect, and the ability to go beyond the exterior to the interior, past a person's disabilities to their abilities. They also need a listening ear, and we need to listen to our business partners.

Parents often don't get talked about enough in this context. They get so tired. The system is so tiring with the paperwork etc. By the time their child has graduated from high school, they have advocated for them countless times. They don't have the energy to push one more detail for their teens and young adults.

When their kids age out of the school system, it presents challenges for the parents. What are the parents going to do with their child while they are working? One young man has a seizure disorder and can't be left alone. They can feel guilty because their child is home alone, or even just that their child is not doing anything productive. Parents can feel bad about themselves.

I think of Ashley's mom. I had taken on the cases of Ashley and her sister because we were just not getting anywhere in our efforts to find them jobs. These girls had been homeschooled since they were eleven or so and had very little experience socializing with others. They had never held down a job. I could see it was important that they got out. Ashley wanted to work in a bakery, and even though I had reservations, I helped place her in one.

Her mom was driving her in to work every morning at 4 a.m., and she was never late.

But unfortunately, Ashley could not do her tasks independently, and within a couple of weeks, she was let go. I talked to her and said, "What lessons are we going to take over to the next job?"

It's not called failure; it's called learning. We learned that she needs support when she is working. The work was far too independent for her. Now we are looking for a fast food or pizza place for her, in a position where she will not work alone.

I have been talking to the girls' mom. I always say it is so important to get to the heart of mom and dad. The parents are usually right. They have had to deal with their children's disabilities for so long. You must also be "shoulder to shoulder" with the parents. So, I collaborate with the mom in Ashley's case. Instead of doing everything myself, I am leaving it in the mom's hands. I want to run with it myself, but she can make those calls of behalf of her daughters.

When the girls are placed, as with any mother of a child with disabilities, their mother's anxiety levels will go down. As mothers, we hope our children will be successful and they will make contributions in the community. For these parents to know their child is fulfilling their God given gifts and purpose in the community is incredible.

Q: What kinds of goals and dreams to do you have for the future in terms of your work at Beyond26?

Ellie: I would like to see us help our jobseekers spiritually. Churches usually don't offer them any kind of programs after youth group ends, and it's hard for them to understand sermons very well. Spiritual gatherings would be high on my list of what I would like to see for our jobseekers. Dreaming big, I would like to see a community develop where community members could support jobseekers on their jobs and living on the weekends, too.

Ellie is also a part of our check-in process. Once a job is found and the jobseeker starts working, our team follows up with both the employer and the jobseekers. Our formula is to check in two times the first month and once a month after until the six-month mark. Quite often the employer will request less calls or to not call after a couple months. Many assure us that they will call if there is a need.

The stories that come out of these check-ins are very encouraging. We realize anew that there are so many benefits that come from employing an individual with a disability. The following two stories were sparked by positive check-ins with our business partners. They are just two out of many jobseekers with whom Ellie has worked closely.

Serena's story starts with a sweet connection to donuts, and even better, Marge's donuts of Marge's Donut Den fame. (Marge's is an iconic donut shop in Grand Rapids). Marge knew Ellie's son in law and mentioned to her that she had a young relative with some mild cognitive disabilities moving to Grand Rapids. Serena and her father had heard that Grand Rapids had more resources and connections for them, and came in search of connection and work, specifically for Serena. She had lived in a Southern state and was quite isolated in her community.

Ellie found a place for Serena at the New Life Thrift Store, a store that benefits the Christian school where she once worked. But first she met with Serena and realized that she was "very able" and had good fine motor coordination. In the course of her work, she must lift items donated to the store, and sort through those items. Her good ability to reason helps her to discern whether an item should be put out for sale or recycled (not every one of our jobseekers could do this). Serena started at two afternoons per week, and now works three afternoons. We've explored the possibility of her also working in the mornings, but she has pushed back on this; mornings would be too much. For Serena, her twelve hours per week are the perfect amount of work and social interaction for her. In addition to sorting donated items, she greets guests at the donation door and fills out a tax receipt for them if they request one.

Serena benefits from the social interaction with customers and coworkers, too. The customers know her by name and chat with her. She has made good friends at work and through attending Beyond26 social events. "She has a social context now," says Ellie, who reports that Serena always comes in to work with a smile, gets the job done, and even better, brings Marge's donuts on a regular basis to share with her coworkers. "Serena is truly a blessing to the New Life Thrift Store," says her boss. "She works hard and always has a positive attitude and smile. She is courteous with the customers. She has grown so much since starting with us. She has been a great addition to our store.

She's loved by her coworkers, who made sure to let us know that they think she is 'such a sweetheart.'" We agree!

***

Michael is a great success story, for us, but more important, for his parents and himself. Born into a family of three boys, Michael and his parents have traveled a long and winding road to get to where he is now: employed full time in a job he loves.

School was very difficult for him and at first, no one knew just why. He was sick often with stomach troubles, which no doctor could identify, and he had a keen sensitivity about his clothing and what types of textures he could tolerate. Add to this some speech difficulties and Ellie was suspicious that he could be on the autism spectrum.

"Mom and dad were beside themselves," says Ellie about Michael's eventual diagnosis. Finally, there were reasons for Michael's issues and behaviors. "The school thought he was getting sick on purpose."

After high school ended, Michael sat on the couch for about ten years. Then he began attending a skills program through Kent County and learned how to change tires. "He was very successful at it," says Ellie. "He loved it." His illnesses, which had been so frequent in high school, lessened, and Michael began a more advanced program in mechanics until he got Covid-19 and was forced to drop out of the program.

Ellie persisted in trying to get Michael placed at a good job, despite this setback. He could still get a job, she figured, even if he couldn't continue with the training. Besides his passion for hunting and fishing, he loved cars and wanted to work on cars in some capacity. Ellie steered him to Wonderland Tires, a tire shop who had hired a couple other jobseekers and had a culture of understanding people with disabilities. The assistant manager had ADHD and had struggled in high school, so he had a soft heart towards anyone who had labored in school. But this was not school—the tire shop was a place where Michael could use his talents in working on cars and succeed.

Because he needed to build stamina and confidence, he started out off part time. Within a week, he was working extra hours. "They need me," he said, and he was right. Michael not only became an essential part of the workplace at Wonderland Tires, but he made friends with his co-workers who shared his enthusiasm for hunting and fishing. He is valued at work, too. "We could use more people like Michael," his boss told me recently.

Like Serena and Michael, our jobseekers are usually excited about finding work that fits them well. Says Ellie, "They have been told no so many times, when they are told yes, it means so much."

Jobseekers such as Serena and Michael are saying yes to life, and a higher quality of life. They hold down a job, get up in the morning, bear responsibilities, and gain confidence. Their lives are reversed, and people like Ellie are a big reason why.

CHAPTER 11

Our Partner J&H Family Stores

One of our strongest business partners is J & H Family Stores, a family-owned chain of forty-five convenience stores all over West Michigan. When I first reached out to Loren, a third-generation owner and J & H's director of retail operations, he wasn't sure what to think about Beyond26. But now that we have successfully placed hardworking jobseekers at his stores, he has become a big supporter of what we do. I'll let him tell you the rest of the story:

"When I first met Denny and Dirk, and they presented the (Beyond26 program), I was a little skeptical about how it was going to work. I thought about our current employees—would they be receptive to working with people who have more needs than most? At first, we hired the initial jobseekers to help the community and do something good, but truthfully, this has worked out to be a benefit for us.

Working with the jobseekers has been such a positive. Bringing in people with different needs and abilities and watching them overcome daily struggles and come to work with positive attitudes, has brought our employee base closer together. Our other employees benefit from helping others; they appreciate their own lives and abilities more. We are blessed to have some managers who take the extra time with the jobseekers. Hiring jobseekers has affected the culture of our company in a good way; there is more of a family feel. It has been very beneficial on the morale side of things.

In a time where we cannot find enough employees, we've got some good workers who help keep our business running well.

Beyond26 is a great organization. They take people who could become afterthoughts in the community and provide them with a sense of purpose and accomplishment they can't find anywhere else. Turning the "me culture" into a "we culture" applies perfectly to what has happened to our company since we began working with these jobseekers. I am grateful."

And we in turn are grateful for J & H. It's great to hear that our employers are realizing benefits from hiring our jobseekers. They are gaining loyal employees who are devoted, who want to be accepted and be part of a team. Our jobseekers gain a community away from home, job skills, and the guidance and friendship of their coworkers and managers.

***

Pictured is our 100th jobseeker placement with his supervisor at J&H Family Stores.

Even though we try and thoroughly vet each jobseeker and determine whether they would be a good fit for a particular company, it doesn't always work out the way we want, at least not at first. You know what they say—if at first you don't succeed, try, try again. This was the case with Cora.

Cora was one of those jobseekers who sputtered out a bit at first, but eventually gained the confidence and stamina to fill her job requirements with strength and skill. When she and her mom came to us, they were in a tough spot. For one reason or another, they had to leave their family home for financial reasons. Cora, who has severe anxiety, depression and even agoraphobia, wanted to help the family with income. She wanted to stock shelves or clean, in a workplace where the people were "friendly." I thought the J & H truck stop near her home would be a good fit,and they needed help. I offered to call the manager and set up an interview, but Cora and her mom took the bull by the horns and applied themselves. She got the job, but that wasn't the end of the story.

The manager had Cora clean the showers which the truck drivers could rent for $6 (including soap and a clean towel). She cleaned two or three showers before it dawned on her that she would have to turn around and clean them again in rapid fashion as more drivers came in to use them. She quit on her first day!

Thankfully, that was not the end of her story, either. When the family got settled in Cora's brother's home in the Walker area outside Grand Rapids—a stopgap measure while they searched for housing—I called Cora back. "Would you be interested in finding work on your new end of town?" She said that she would be interested, and an opportunity soon opened. As it turned out, another job seeker, Doug, had been doing such a good job at his J & H location on Walker Ave. that a nearby J & H store heard about it. They called me to see if I had any jobseekers in the area who would be interested in working at their store. Providentially, Doug lives in an apartment which was located two buildings away from the J & H on Remembrance Road. Since it would be extremely convenient for him to work there, he took that job opening, leaving an opening at the Walker Ave. store near Cora!

Before Cora interviewed there, I had a talk with the manager, assuring her that all Cora needed was some positive affirmations. This turned out to be true, as Cora has flourished in her new job. Mondays, Wednesdays and Fridays from noon to four involve bagging ice, sweeping floors, stocking shelves, cleaning bathrooms, stocking the freezer and making sure everything looks nice. Allie, Cora's manager, is typical of J & H managers, who are often moms who show a lot of affirmation and love to our jobseekers. "We all love Cora here and she's come so far," says Allie. "Cora has been a godsend to our team here at Walker. She's a hard worker who pushes past her own comfort zone and amazes me daily." Cora's mom reports that she has learned some coping strategies and has expanded beyond her twelve hours a week at work to go out more often to shop and eat. Like many of our jobseekers, working has allowed her to develop socially, too.

***

Kallie lives in a rural area about half an hour from Grand Rapids. She has severe ADD along with some cognitive impairments. She graduated from high school three or four years before we met her, having taken some modified classes. When she came to us, referred by Allegan County Community Mental Health

Services, Kallie had never held down a job. In the years since she had graduated, Kallie's only work experience was painting curbs for her hometown (a work experience program), babysitting her nieces and nephews, and chicken sitting for neighbors.

When Kallie filled out our paperwork, she noted that her skills included a good sense of humor and the ability to follow instructions. She was interested in a job stocking shelves and running a cash register. I pinned her location on Google and did a search of nearby businesses. The closest was a J & H Family Store at a nearby exit. When I called the store manager to see if they had any openings, they said they could use someone like Kallie, and an interview was set up for her. I couldn't go to the interview with Kallie, so Emily, my development director, who was new at the time, went along. The supervisor who interviewed Kallie said the interview had gone well, and that her supervisor, the HR director for J & H, had okayed Kallie working there twenty hours a week.

Kallie's job entails stocking shelves and custodial duties. She is also being trained on the cash register; she is a natural with the customers. Says Kallie's boss, Angela: "Kallie has a delightful personality. She has grown here! We think of her as part of our family. She walks around with a smile, positive attitude, joking personality and completes her work before she leaves."

***

Jay is one of my best-loved jobseeker stories. If you and I met on vacation and you asked me to tell you about Beyond26 and its people and culture, I would tell you about Jay.

In May of 2017, then 17-year-old Jay was cruising down a hill on his motorcycle when he hit a pothole, flew over the handlebars, and hit his bare head on a curb. He was given a less than 2% chance to live through the experience. Three months in a coma was followed by months of rehabilitation. "For him to walk and be able to do what he does is huge," said his stepmom, Emily. "He was supposed to be in a wheelchair."

Incredibly, Jay can walk with an uneven gait and using a cane sometimes. One of his two arms is basically locked. But despite these big challenges, Jay has a powerful desire to work. Thankfully, it did not take us long to place Jay in a worksite. Other organizations had not been able to place him in a job, but I was determined to do so. I did the same thing as with Kallie and Googled businesses around his home. Within a month of being in our program, he ended up working part time at a J & H Family Stores location in Dorr, Michigan, nearby his home. This has been a great success story according to Jay, his family, and his employer.

"I wish I had ten more Jays," said Shelly, Jay's manager at J & H. "He comes to work with a great personality every day. He's fun and he likes to talk to everybody. He likes to work! He's got a really great sense of humor and keeps us laughing a little bit every day."

At J&H, Jay's jobs range from keeping on top of the garbage bags at various gas pumps, bagging ice and other cleaning duties.

His manager Shelly says this is the first time she has had to manage somebody with this level of disabilities. "I was more concerned about safety issues, but we got him situated with his own cart," she said. "He always tells me when he can't do something and needs help."

She adds that J & H's ability to find special connections to the community drew her to work for them. "People that can't do very well in normal situations have the chance to get out there and work and mingle with people."

 Mingling with people is Jay's favorite part of the job. That and getting paid.

"For him to get his first paycheck—he was so excited," said Emily. "It's giving him that step closer to independence. He has this drive; most people don't have it. He wants to earn his own money and be independent. That's what we wanted from the start. It's crazy that he's come so far. I am proud of him."

Jay is proud of himself, too. His advice to disabled people looking for a job? "Be persistent. People like me just want to work and prove to people they can work." At the time of this writing, Jay just celebrated his one-year anniversary at work.

"Jay is part of the team," said Shelly. "We really enjoy him."

CHAPTER 12

Success Stories, Part 2

Job seekers are often tucked away from sight, sitting on a couch for five, ten, and even twenty years. As Loren Hoppen from J & H Family Stores said, these young adults with disabilities can easily become afterthoughts in their communities. They can be hidden away from society, their gifts and potential buried.

But a job changes everything. It gives our jobseekers that all-important routine as well as a community outside their families. Good work confers dignity and purpose where there was once a feeling of meaninglessness.

Jeremy sat on a couch for twenty years until his mom and dad died. In his case and others, we have seen parents who coddle their children with disabilities. Unintentionally, they may place limitations on their jobseeker's ability. "Oh, my Johnny could never hold down a job!" they think. But Johnny—and Jeremy—can and do exceed expectations.

Jeremy's brother brought him in to us and said he would love to be doing something productive. It just so happened that Jeremy, who has autism, knew the Dewey Decimal System, a library classification system which allows new books to be added to a library in their appropriate location based on subject. It's still used in some libraries, and Jeremy had once helped in his school library back in the day.

Wonderfully, we were able to place Jeremy at his local library, putting books away for ten hours per week. It's ever satisfying to be able to prove to a jobseeker and his community that they *can* work and contribute to society. Jobseekers discover that the limitations once placed upon them are no longer valid or can be overcome with the help of patient employers and coworkers.

I think of Ethan (also autistic), one of our early jobseekers who was our first hire at Meijer Distribution Center where he worked picking orders in a warehouse. His job entailed walking down the vast rows of boxes at the warehouse, each one marked with a number and a letter, say 2a and 7b. He wore a computer on his wrist, which held instructions for which sporting good or clothing item etc. each store wanted. His computer might say "10 2a's" and "15 7b's" for example, and Ethan would have to fill a tub with things he had picked to fulfill that store's order. Multiple coworkers helped him get to the point where he could pick orders at the correct speed, until he grew into his role and exemplified that he could be timely and complete. Eventually, Ethan was proud to be promoted to the pharmacy room where he picks more detailed orders for Meijer pharmacies.

Ethan's story is just another example of how teamwork assists a jobseeker in overcoming their limitations. Way to go, Ethan and Meijer!

***

Remember Riley, one of our jobseekers at Beyond26 document shredding mentioned earlier in the book? He loved to ride along with Herb and help him on his route, partially because he could usually get Herb to stop for donuts on the way back. One day I stopped Riley and told him he could get a job beyond document shredding. "You've got such an outgoing personality," I said.

With that little nudge of encouragement, Riley spotted a job opening at a local gas station/convenience store by his house, applied for and got a job. I knew there was a risk to this move. At Riley's meet and greet, he confessed that he had a problem with stealing. (One of the things I love about our jobseekers is their transparency.) One of our administrative assistants, whom we call Taz, made him a laminated card that says, "I will not steal" as well as the Bible verse Exodus 20:15: "Thou shalt not steal." Riley keeps that card on him, as a reminder when temptations came up. He had already stolen from Walmart and had to perform community service. He did not want to go through that again.

Working at a gas station brought new temptations that did not exist at Beyond26 document shredding, but Riley was determined to stick to his principles and his goal not to steal.

One day, his boss, Laura, got called away from her desk and had to help someone out back. Riley walked by her office and saw the door open, no boss Laura, and cash on her desk. "I was really tempted," he said. Riley went to another employee and said "I have a problem with Laura's door being open because there is money on her desk. Can you please close her door?" He faced and overcame his temptation, which is a testament to how much he values his work and the trust of his boss and coworkers. He loves his job.

"You know what the best part of my job is?" he asked me one day. "I get to empty the trash and my boss lets me keep all the cans and bottles I find to turn them in for a can return cash refund."

His employers appreciate and value him, too. "We all love Riley's sense of humor and his great taste in music," said his boss, Laura. "He loves 80's and 90's music and sometimes sings along with the music as he works. He loves to tell very corny jokes which we all love and laugh at."

***

Families of our jobseekers are affected in a positive way as well. Once an individual with a disability finds a work community that cares for them, it influences family life. The comments and notes we receive tell the story. Here's one from our jobseeker Madison's mother:

"Wanted to quickly reach out to say THANK YOU again for the assistance with connecting Madison to her new job at Fire Rock Grille. Things seem to be going well and she is coming home tired and happy each day.... praise God! I had recently emailed her supervisor to help iron out a pay roll kink (they had her account # down incorrectly), and he mentioned that they really enjoy having her and she's catching on well with everything, so that was awesome to hear! I felt this was worth a quick email to celebrate a success and send up some praise!"

Madison was one of Ellie's students who found unlikely joy in a job some would consider beneath them. At her meet and greet, she was very specific about what kind of job she wanted. "I'd like to work with a team and load a dishwasher or do other types of cleaning."

Emily, our development director, and communications coordinator heard that Madison wanted a job washing dishes. Emily's boyfriend worked at Fire Rock Grille, a restaurant inside a country club, and she knew that they were looking for a dishwasher. Within two or three days, Madison was being interviewed and then hired for her position at the restaurant. She's been at her job for about six months, working fifteen to twenty hours per week. To me, Madison is a great success story. We will often suggest kitchen work to our jobseekers, and they don't want to do it. But for Madison, the job fits her well; she absolutely loves it!

Elana, who is autistic, came to us as someone who had been working and active already, but her current job didn't suit her. Elana was working for her grandmother at a five and dime store, and while she enjoyed it, she wanted to work in a greenhouse, ideally with people her own age. We were able to place her at Horrocks, a West Michigan institution, which is part greenhouse, part upscale grocery and wine store. Elana quickly learned that she struggled to work in the greenhouse because of the heat and humidity. She nestled into the role of cashier, a role in which she thrives. One of our staff got her a neck cooling fan, which blows cold air into her face and keeps her cool on the hottest days. And she is making friends with her coworkers.

Recently, Elana's mom wrote us a note about how she thinks her daughter's job is going:

"Elana is doing amazing at Horrocks; it is very busy. She loves it though and is handling it quite well. It is nice to see her interacting with people her own age. She is getting about forty hours every two weeks, which is perfect. She is handling eight hour shifts great. Any more hours and it would be too much. Elana is quite a different person since working there. She is positive, upbeat. I feel like she knows how needed she is there. She is being productive and making great money. I cannot thank you all enough for staying with it and getting her a position out there. I am so grateful for you and the work that you do at Beyond 26, you have blessed my daughter with an awesome new life!"

CHAPTER 13

Flourishing Together, Shoulder to Shoulder

Since we began Beyond26 four years ago, we have placed one hundred and two jobseekers, thirty-nine in 2021 alone. In 2022, we are shooting for a goal of placing fifty job seekers. We do one to two meet and greets per week, on average, and field several inquiries per week, but it will take more than one job developer to process this number of people through the system. We are in the process of hiring another job developer to focus on cultivating new business partners to employ our jobseekers. We celebrated our 100th jobseeker placement in March of 2022.

We currently have nine paid employees, which includes two full time employees, seven part-time, and five volunteers in both our Grand Rapids base and our new document shredding operation in Grand Haven, Michigan.

My son Dirk III thinks our simple concept and system can be replicated across America and throughout the world! Personally, I would like to see a Beyond26 regional office throughout Michigan within the next five years. I dream that every Transitions program within a county would be assigned to not only the resources available through State organizations but also their regional Beyond26 office. Our support guide and experience could help make this reality everywhere.

Forty-five business partners stand shoulder to shoulder with us, partnering with us to employ our jobseekers. Our initial budget in 2019 was our first donation from a charitable trust of $31,000. Since hiring a development director in 2021, our giving turned the corner as we become more noticeable to "funders," as they like to be called. Just a few days ago, we received an anonymous check for $15,000 with a note in the memo line reading "jobseeker sponsorships." Our budget for 2022 is ten times what it was in those early days.

I am so grateful when I review these numbers. It humbles me to see how people have responded to our vision in terms of donations and delights me to know that 90% of the jobseekers we have placed are still working. But it has never been about numbers. It's always been about helping individuals with disabilities find work, find community, and find routine. As Executive Director, my job is the same now as it was at the beginning, I have 4 pipelines to fill – Jobseekers, Business Partners, Volunteers and Donors.

People always ask us what our fee is, and I love to tell them there is no fee. We want to be totally accessible to anyone who wants our help. Part of the reason we can keep this system simple is the fact we do not need to answer to a state or federal Agency. This creates fiscal efficiencies that allow us to stretch a dollar. Private business, individual donors and funders can make this happen. Where will Beyond26 grow next?

Truthfully, this is a unique program. In my initial research, I found only a couple of likeminded programs nationwide, one in Denver and one in Seattle. And of course, not every state had a Dr. Charles Mange to legislate on behalf of young adults with disabilities. Fifty years ago, he introduced legislation that was signed into law a program which would provide quality education for young adults with disabilities to the age of twenty-six.

In many states, these individuals age out of the school system much earlier. I got a call recently from two brothers, one with a disability, from Austin, Texas. In Texas, young adults age out at twenty-two (in many states it is eighteen!). I gladly sent the brothers our support guide and wished them well. It would be amazing if the Beyond26 vision caught fire in other states, and people could launch their own "Beyond22" or whatever they wanted to call it. That is my dream, that is what keeps me energized for the next day, week, month, and the years to come.

***

What does work mean to a jobseeker? I have been surprised how much a job can mean. Imagine a routine where you get up in the morning with no destination, day after day. Maybe we can relate because of the Covid-19 pandemic. We were cooped up for over a year. No work destination, no social outlet, no church, and no interaction with friends.

I believe every position, from a two hour per week volunteer gig to a full-time job, provides value to a jobseeker. They are proud and pleased to be able to contribute to society in whatever capacity possible. Community, friendships, inclusion, purpose, dignity, and happiness are the byproducts of employment.

Meeting our jobseeker right where they are is exactly the correct method. The job must match the jobseeker. Some jobseekers are significantly challenged, but for them, even two hours per week shredding documents means the world to them. Others can do more. One of our jobseekers is autistic and is interning with a computer programming firm. Another college graduate is aiming for a full-time job in environmental biology. Many are working twenty-forty hours a week at grocery stores and convenience stores. Cleaning offices, shredding paper, folding clothes at a thrift store, working at a warehouse distribution center—our list of jobseeker positions is growing.

Jobs provide completion for our jobseekers. They are proud to be working and are loyal to their employers. This how life is meant to be.

***

We envision a community where every individual can enjoy the benefits of a workplace environment, and in turn every workplace is able to celebrate different abilities and enjoy the benefits of inclusivity. How will our mission change our communities? One key is that it will become normal for us to see people with disabilities in the workplace.

Do you remember as a kid you would see someone with a physical or cognitive disability and stare, to the point your mom might tell you to stop staring? As a kid, it was hard not to stare because you had not seen someone like that before. This is a reality in the workforce as well. We are not used to seeing individuals with disabilities working shoulder to shoulder with others. In time, as more and more individuals with disabilities are involved and working in our communities the stares will stop and it will be ordinary and unremarkable to work with, eat with and socialize with our coworkers who have disabilities.

When an employer and a team join in helping an individual with a disability it changes the trajectory and culture of the company and the community. In his book *No Greatness without Goodness: How a Father's Love Changed a Company and Sparked a Movement,*

Randy Lewis says inclusivity changes company cultures from being a "Me" culture to a "We" culture. The more this happens, the more it will be normal. The more normal it is, a me culture turns into a we culture, and we focus on helping each other and getting work done together. Team members that support each other become advocates for each other. Employers will find avid employees who want to work; once they have a work community, they don't call in sick. Our employers are getting loyal employees. Yes, a me culture is changed to a we culture! Randy Lewis proved it at Walgreens Distributions Centers, and Beyond26 is proving it in West Michigan.

***

Joel and Mel are living this dream. Joel, a jobseeker with Down Syndrome, likes to call his sister and report he will be home right after having lunch with the boss. Joel comes in on Tuesdays and Fridays to clean Mel's insurance agency office near his home. Joel has a great sense of humor and makes Mel laugh. A friendship has developed, and now Mel takes Joel out for a hamburger every Friday after his shift.

You could even say Joel feels like his workplace is his home away from home. One Tuesday after Joel's shift, Mel found Joel napping on the couch in the employee lounge. Mel thought it was the best thing ever that Joel felt that comfortable. Whereas Joel could've been spending way too much time on his couch at home, he became a valuable team member, and even better, a friend. That is community, that is inclusion, and that is the way it is supposed to be.

***

We chose our core verse for Beyond26 very carefully, finally arriving at 2 Corinthians 8:13-14. "No, you're shoulder to shoulder with them all the way, your surplus matching their deficit, their surplus matching your deficit. In the end you come out even." (*The Message*).

To me, this verse exemplifies what we intend to do with Beyond26, coming together, shoulder to shoulder, with one person's strength filling another person's lack. I'd like to see strong individuals help others who don't have the same strengths. The Madison's of this world are willing to wash dishes, while others want to cook or run the business end of the restaurant. If we can all do our jobs, we can all win, working together to find success and flourishing. Slowly but surely, Beyond26 is helping change people's lives for the better.

CHAPTER 14

Full Circle

When I started writing The Beyond26 Story, my son Will was still in school and it caught me by surprise when the Beyond26 mission began to serve my family, and my son Will. The Beyond26 story has come full circle.

When Phyllis and I were discussing whether to adopt Will, we calculated how old we would be when he aged out of the school system. I would be 67 and Phyllis 64 years old. Realizing we were not going to be spring chickens anymore, the decision to adopt was a risk.

We accepted the risk and have now seen our family unit mature and succeed. Will is working everyday (more to come later in this chapter), his sister Leah works for her brothers, and we all have a routine that includes family at home as well as at work. Will bowls, plays Pokemon, listens to music and alternates between playing guitars, drums and keyboard to the YouTube videos he watches. Life is consistent and good!

Will and his best friend Nick have been shredding documents every summer and during some of the holiday breaks. They work well together, always sharing a machine and keeping the hum of the paper shredder active with a steady rhythm.

Lunch time includes a trip to the vending machine to purchase a pop (soda) to wash down their food. Their routine is predictable and familiar.   A familiar routine that suits them uniquely.

Having Down Syndrome, Will's main disabilities include some cognitive, but his main disability is verbal. Speech is difficult for him. One-word answers at best.

Nick, however, is verbal and can understand Will's speech and body language. Nick has more physical disabilities than cognitive. He has one lame arm and wears a brace on his left leg.

What is remarkable is how they anticipate each other's needs. If Nick has a soda with a screw-off cap, Will knows to open it for him. Tying off a bag of shredded paper is impossible for Nick, so Will knows how to do that job for him. Nick in turn knows how to speak up for Will when there is a question or problem. He also is an encourager when Will gets lazy or unmotivated. That is something Nick does not struggle with! He has an incredible work ethic.

I often refer to the two of them as "Yeng and Yang". One man's deficiency is covered by the other man. Together they rock! It ties in so well with Beyond26's key verse from II Corinthians 8:12-14 MSG, "No, you are shoulder to shoulder with them all the way, your surplus matching their deficit, their surplus matching your deficit. In the end you come out even." In everyday life it is much the same. If I need the auto mechanic to fix my car, he in turn needs me to be his customer so he can earn a living.

The summer of 2022 was a pivotal summer for us. What changed? A local business, Weller Truck Parts, approached Beyond26 to get involved in our program. At the time we did not know whether this was financial sponsorship or anything else. What they had decided as a leadership team is that they wanted inclusion of individuals with disabilities in their workforce. In the meeting that presented that opportunity, I questioned whether this could be a work site for Nick and Will.

After the meeting, I contacted their HR person and asked a simple question, "would you be willing to give my son Will and his buddy Nick a 6-shift internship so you can evaluate their abilities? The six shifts would bring them to the start of school and if there are positive outcomes, could they be invited back next summer?"

It took a little while for them to respond and I was having doubts it was going to happen. The positive response did come! So, we set up their trial shifts. One of the Beyond26 job coaches joined Nick and Will for the first 2 shifts and deemed they were ready to go on their own. I asked her to do one more shift to make sure, but after a couple hours she called me and reassured me the "boys" had it all under control.

After their initial 6 shifts, Page from HR called me in and said it all went well. Will and Nick worked hard. It was satisfying to me to hear this. My son and his friend succeeded and are appreciated! The next question asked caught me off guard. They asked if Will and Nick could stay on staff permanently! I explained that they both are in school yet and I expected them not to be able to work and go to school. I asked the school system whether they could both work and attend school. The school administrator said the whole point of transition services is to help their students land a job. The school wrote the job right into their Individualized Education Plan (IEP).

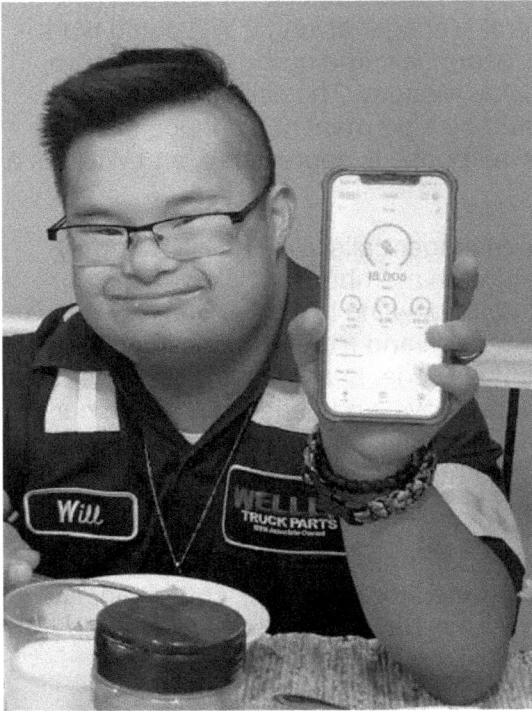

Will and Nick work from 9-2 PM every Wednesday and Thursday. On the other weekdays they attend Kent ISU Transition classes. Loving their routine, they also bowl in a challenger bowling league in the spring and fall. Will plays in a challenger softball league as well, attends church with us and has a routine he loves. Nick's parents have told me they never anticipated Nick acquiring a job and are so thankful for the help from Beyond26 to secure this job.

In 2023 Will graduated from the Transitions program and added a third day to his routine. On Fridays he works by himself, going through his routine of straightening tables and chairs, cleaning tabletops, microwaves, vending machines, drinking fountains and cleaning bathrooms. He averages between 15,000-19,000 steps every day. Physically his doctor says for him to keep up the good work. His blood pressure and heart rate are perfect!

In 2024 Nick graduated from the Transitions program and added a day to his routine. He works Mondays on his own. In my eyes, what is so encouraging is the independence these young men are embracing. I am so proud!

In October of 2024 the Beyond26 Document shredding program ran out of documents to shred so we closed the program for one week. Since Will volunteers there every Monday and Tuesday we had to explain the situation to him. In the process of explaining to him, Will indicated he wanted to go to Weller Truck Parts instead. I asked if he would like to work every day at Weller Truck Parts, giving up his spot at Beyond26 Document Shredding. I explained that it may not be an option, but I would check with the General Manager. I texted the General Manager asking if Will could work Monday and Tuesday. His response came quickly. He said sure, send Will into work, I'll call you Monday. The call came and we discussed whether this could be a permanent work position. The General Managers positive response is appreciated, and Will has a permanent job he loves!

Weller Truck Parts General Manager calls Will and Nick "family" and treats them like all their team members. A fellow team member attends Nick and Will's bowling league events as well as Will's softball games. He calls Will and Nick a "hoot" and builds their confidence as well as their pride. Both Nick's family and ours are thankful for the acceptance, love, and patience given to our sons. We have been told Will and Nick have a positive influence on their company culture. Another example of supporting a "we" rather than a "me" culture.

All in all, a job is changing the community we live in. Will is recognized outside of work at the store, the mall, church and in our community. One job at a time, Beyond26 hopes to continue touching the lives of our jobseekers and their families! As of December 2024, we have placed 240 jobseekers in jobs throughout the community with 110 participating businesses. May I help you get a Beyond26 started in your community? Contact me! I'm here to help!

Dirk

Appendix Support Team Guide

I included the Beyond26 Support Team Guide materials as an appendix to my book because of inspiration from another author that shared his knowledge of business leadership without holding back. I believe that sharing this information will inspire someone else to start a non-profit like Beyond26 in their community. That could be a community initiative or a church project. If they follow the steps in our guide, they can be successful!

Two people spent a lot of time developing this guidebook. Emily Voorhees, Beyond26's first fulltime team member is our communications specialist as well as our development director. She fulfilled both aspects of her role plus put this guide together in less than a year. Ellie VanKeulen is not only a board member but also an active volunteer. She did our first 50 meet and greets and helped Emily refine and edit the Support Team Guide. Thanks to both of you for your great work.

Some of our process and systems were taken from the booklet "Putting Faith to Work" that created by the Collaborative of Faith and Disabilities, sponsored by the Kessler Foundation and led by Bill Gaventa and Erik Carter. You can read more about them at https://faithanddisability.org/. Thank you for an outline that we were able to adapt outside of a church setting. Our community is blessed by it!

The Beyond26 Team Support Guide has been developed over time. This guide outlines what works for us at the current time. I think all processes change over time and imagine ours will too. Take it and use to influence your community to include individuals with disabilities in their workplaces. Inclusion changes lives for the better. Businesses, families, team members, group homes and especially our jobseekers benefit from jobs in their community. How can I help you get on the bandwagon? Feel free to reach out any time. https://beyondtwentysix.org.

Beyond261

SUPPORT TEAM GUIDE

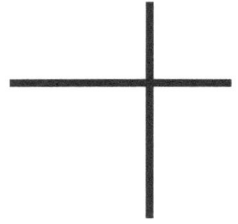

TABLE OF CONTENTS

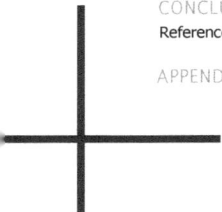

INTRODUCTION

Beyond26 began in 2018, in Grand Rapids, Michigan, by a group of community members who noticed a lack of opportunities for individuals with disabilities over the age of 26. This group was comprised of parents of adult children with disabilities and individuals deeply connected to these families. They understood that 26 is a critical age; this is the age of discovery, and also the year they age out of Michigan's education system. While the next step should likely be employment, those opportunities were, unfortunately, few and far between. The group then set to work bridging that gap between local businesses and a community of jobseekers through employment and volunteer opportunities.

This support guide detail that process for those who would seek to implement it in their own communities.

> **"**
> Our goal is to facilitate expanding the community circle for our job applicants. When they start school, they have a small community circle... and it expands until they hit the end of high school. And then they go into the transition phase, and it begins to contract... Their need for both work and social community is strong.
>
> BOB WONDERGEM,
> *BOARD PRESIDENT*

PUTTING FAITH TO WORK

Portions of the information in this Support Guide have been adapted from the *"Putting Faith to Work"* Model[1] which was created in collaboration by four University Centers for Excellence in Developmental Disabilities. This model utilized research-based strategies to connect people with disabilities to quality employment opportunities through natural networks and to provide other individualized support.

MISSION, VISION, AND VALUES

MISSION

Our mission is to find employment & volunteer opportunities for individuals with disabilities, ages eighteen and up.

VISION

We envision a community standing "shoulder to shoulder," where our jobseekers' unique skills and abilities are valued, and they are able to enjoy the full benefits of a work community. In turn, everyworkplace is able to enjoy the benefits of a diverse and inclusive workforce.

VALUES

We aim to demonstrate the love and support of Jesus Christ as we work with individuals throughout the employment process.

> You're shoulder to shoulder with them all the way, your surplus matching their deficit, their surplus matching your deficit. In the end, you come out even.
>
> *II Corinthian s 8:12-14 (MSG)*

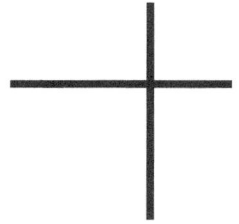

DEFINING SUPPORT TEAM ROLES

INTAKE SPECIALIST

The intake specialist will conduct all meet & greets and is responsible for all documentation and records leading up to the pre-employment services. Depending on staffing, the intake specialist's duties could also be performed by the job developer or administrative assistant. For the purposes of this support guide, the responsibilities will be separated.

JOB DEVELOPER

The job developer will find employment opportunities for the jobseekers and provide all pre- and post-employment support services and respective documentation. They will also work to maintain and grow a network of area businesses that partner with Beyond26 through community outreach and advocacy. One or more of the job developer duties may be performed by a volunteer job advocate based on the volunteer's preferences.

PRAYER PARTNER (VOLUNTEER)

A prayer partner is a volunteer recipient of the prayer list (See pg. 28), who prays for the support and success of the jobseekers.

JOB COACH

A job coach can be a paid or volunteer position that will work on- and off-site to provide direct support to an employed jobseeker who needs additional assistance performing their job responsibilities or adjusting to a work environment. See pg. 15 for more information.

CHARACTERISTICS OF A JOBSEEKER'S TEAM[2]

ENTHUSIASTIC

Successful team members are committed to our mission and display energy and enthusiasm for their work. Being able to communicate enthusiasm to the jobseeker (and each other) sets an example to be positive on the job.

RESPECTFUL AND RESPONSIVE

Team members establish rapport with others. They listen sincerely, respect other's thoughts, and respond to the jobseeker at his or her age level.

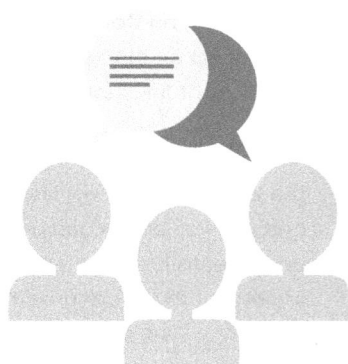

FLEXIBLE

Team members are adaptable. They try to eliminate, adjust, or change how they are teaching/coaching/interacting to match the capabilities of the jobseeker (and other) or job site constraints.

SENSE OF HUMOR

Having a sense of humor and demonstrating that it's okay when things don't always go as planned is important. Laughing and smiling about things that have gone wrong sends the message that it's okay to make mistakes as long as you learn from them.

SINCERE AND HONEST

Successful team members don't fake it; they deal with their jobseekers (and each other) in a straightforward manner. It's important to admit mistakes and model how to find answers to questions.

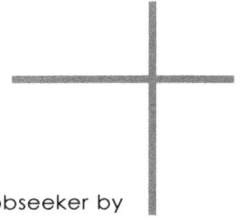

PROMOTE CONFIDENTIALITY

Team members will seek to maintain the confidentiality of the jobseeker by sharing information only with Beyond26 team members and job site team members to promote privacy and respect. Staff and volunteers should adhere to HIPAA policies (Health Insurance Portability Accountability Act).

EMBODY LOVE

Team members will seek to embody Jesus' command to, "Love others as well as you love yourself." (MSG) "Love is patient, love is kind...it always protects, always trusts, always hopes, always perseveres." I Corinthians 13:4-7(NIV)

WHAT YOU WILL NEED

CUSTOMER RELATIONSHIP MANAGEMENT (CRM)

A database for managing all of your relationships and interactions with jobseekers, caregivers, business partners, donors, and volunteers.

SUPPORT TEAM RESOURCES FOLDER

All documents needed to perform the services described in this support guide can be found in the Google folder titled "Support Team Resources." This includes all appendix materials. Some documents are samples and will need to be modified to reflect your organization or branch of Beyond26.

MEETING PLACE

A secure meeting place should be established to conduct Meet & Greets and support services. If a permanent location is not available, consider reserving conference rooms at a local library.

PRINTER AND FILE CABINET

Many jobseeker-related documents will require hard copies. A readily available printer and secure filing cabinet are strongly recommended.

NEW JOBSEEKER
ACTION PLAN

The following is a step-by-step breakdown of the process following a jobseeker-initiated request for services.

1   INTAKE SPECIALIST CONTACTS JOBSEEKER (OR PRIMARY CONTACT) TO SET UP MEET & GREET (M&G)

2   INTAKE SPECIALIST COMPLETES ALL M&G PREPARATORY TASKS

3   INTAKE SPECIALIST AND JOB DEVELOPER (OPTIONAL) CONDUCT MEET & GREET AND COMPLETE DOCUMENTATION

4   JOB DEVELOPER PERFORMS PRE-EMPLOYMENT SUPPORT SERVICES (IF APPLICABLE)

5   JOB DEVELOPER OR JOB ADVOCATE UTILIZE NETWORK AND OUTREACH METHODS TO SECURE EMPLOYMENT OR VOLUNTEER OPPORTUNITY

6   JOB DEVELOPER COMPLETES POST-EMPLOYMENT DOCUMENTATION, AND SUPPORT SERVICES (IF APPLICABLE)

7   JOB DEVELOPER CONDUCTS AND DOCUMENTS FOLLOW-UP COMMUNICATION WITH JOBSEEKER

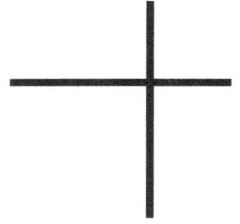

THE MEET & GREET

The purpose of the Meet & Greet (M&G) is to listen to the hopes and dreams of the jobseeker while determining potential job sites based on their skills, necessary accommodations, and personality.

This section will break down the responsibilities of the intake specialist before, during, and after the M&G. From the steps below, the following deliverables should be produced: (1) the completed jobseeker profile, (2) the completed jobseeker resume, (3) an updated prayer list (See pg. 28), and (4) the signed Release of Information form. See Appx A for a compiled checklist.

> No matter what our abilities, goals matter.
>
> - Dirk Bakhuyzen, *Executive Director and Co-Founder*

BEFORE THE MEET & GREET

Following a jobseeker-initiated request for services:

Step One: The intake specialist contacts the jobseeker or their primary contact to acquire:
- The jobseeker's first and last name, phone number, email address, and preferred method of contact.
- Establish M&G time and date

Step Two: Immediately after scheduling the M&G, the intake specialist will:
- Enter the jobseeker's information into the CRM database
- Reserve room for the M&G (if applicable)
- Enter M&G date on calendar and invite other staff members as needed

Step Three: The intake specialist will send a reminder email or phone call one business day prior to the M&G.

DURING THE MEET & GREET

The intake specialist will conduct the M&G, along with the job developer (optional). The intake specialist will want to have the following materials ready before the M&G begins:

* Beyond26 pamphlet and M&G flyer for jobseeker (See pg. 28)
* Blank profile and resume pulled up on computer (See Appxs B & C)
* One hard copy of each question guide printed for interviewer and jobseeker (See Appxs D & E)
* Release of Information (ROI) form (See pg. 28)
* Water bottle for the jobseeker

> The process was simplified from anything else I have tried. I just talked to them and they started looking through what I said that my interests were.
>
> - Darian, Employed Jobseeker[3]

Once the M&G commences, the intake specialist will provide the jobseeker or caregiver with the Beyond26 pamphlet and M&G flyer and will give them a brief overviewof the process. The intake specialist will makesure that the jobseeker knows that this is not an interview, but a 'get-to-know-you' session. Next, the intake specialist will distribute a question guide (See Appx E) to the jobseeker and walk through it while taking notes of the jobseeker's responses.

The final step of the M&G process is to take a photo of the jobseeker and have them fill out and sign the ROI form.

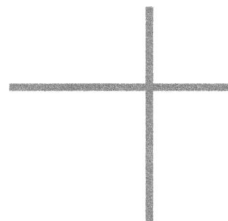

HONORING JOBSEEKER DREAMS

A large part of the mission is to take into consideration the dreams and goals of the jobseeker. From floristry to voice-acting, it can sometimes feel like a tall order to keep dreams in mind and be realistic at the same time. After all, most people don't get their dream job. However, we know that no matter our abilities, dreams matter. There is always a way to factor in the goals and interests of the jobseeker.

For example, in the instance of the voice-acting dream, the jobseeker did not need a paid position. So he began his own podcast with our help, and had it published by a local news company![4] The jobseeker who wanted to work with flowers did need paid work, so she got a job at a local grocery store with a large garden center.

It's just a matter of having straightforward discussions with the jobseeker about how long they are willing to wait for employment, whether or not they need to be paid or receive a certain number of hours, and how flexible they are with compromising certain aspects of their job search.

> If you want a dream job in life, go out and accomplish it. Don't give up on your dream – always reach for the stars!
>
> - Joe, *Beyond26 Jobseeker and Host of "Infinity and Beyond26" Podcast*

AFTER THE MEET & GREET

After the M&G, the intake specialist will use the answers on the question guide to fill out a profile and resume for the jobseeker. Please see Appx F for a sample completed profile. The intake specialist will then complete the following:

- Share a digital copy of the FULL completed profile and resume with the Executive Director and any other pertinent staff

- Share a digital copy of pages 1 & 2 of the profile and resume with the jobseeker/caregiver and ask if there are any necessary changes

- Upload the profile, resume, and ROI form to the jobseeker's CRM database record. Include any new information in the CRM record.

- Add all hard copies of the profile, resume, and ROI form to the filing cabinet

- Update the prayer list to include new jobseeker

Once all of the above steps are completed, the job developer or job advocate will offer pre-employment support services (if applicable).

Simultaneously, the search for employment or volunteer opportunities begins!

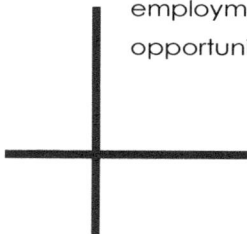

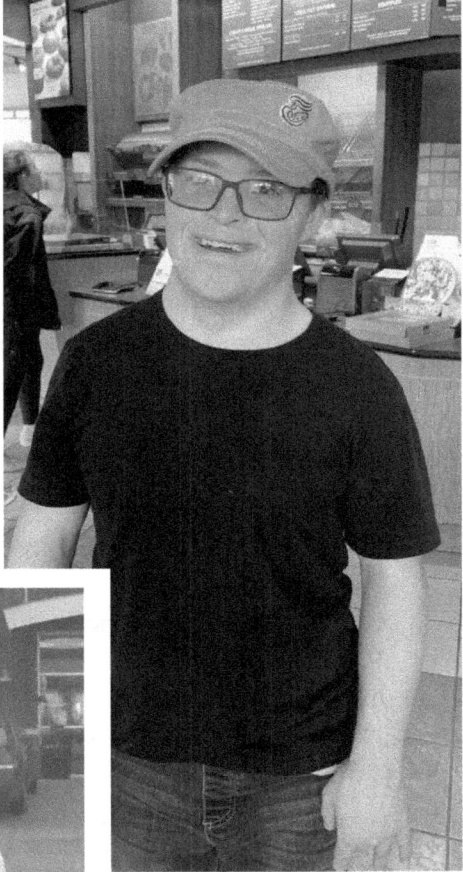

PRE-EMPLOYMENT SERVICES

The purpose of the pre-employment services is to provide support before the jobseeker is hired in order to promote job readiness and prepare for job retention. The pre-employment services needed by each jobseeker can be determined by reviewing the "supports that help my success" section of the jobseeker's profile.

This section will break down three of the optional pre-employment services: (1) reviewing basic job readiness skills, (2) job coaching, and (3) practicing interviews.

REVIEWING BASIC JOB READINESS

For many jobseekers, this will be their first job. The job developer will want to identify any concerns that the jobseeker may have about job readiness. Sometimes this is just a matter of discussing appropriate workplace etiquette such as attendance and dress code policies. For some jobseekers, you may need to get more specific about what parts of a job are a "yes" and what parts are a "no," such as:

- Are they able to read a list of instructions?
- Are they able to count money?
- Are they computer literate?
- Are they able to lift heavy weights?

All of these questions will help define job readiness and help the job developer find the right placement.

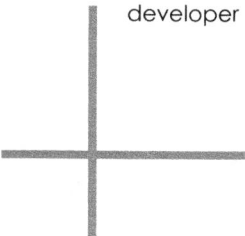

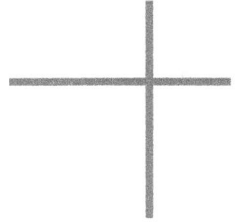

PRACTICING INTERVIEWS

In many cases the jobseeker will have no experience with interviews. Mock interviews are a great way to let the jobseeker practice and build confidence. Practice answers to questions like:

- Can you tell me about yourself?
- What is your experience with [job responsibility]?
- Why do you want to work here?

Mock interviews provide the jobseeker with a chance to talk about what to expect. The job developer will want to discuss topics like what clothes to wear, and they will also want to remind the jobseeker of how important it is to be themselves and answer questions honestly. The employer should already have viewed the jobseeker's profile and be aware of any necessary accommodations before the jobseeker attends the interview to ensure a positive reception.

Often, the jobseeker may want the job developer to attend the interview with them. This is encouraged! There are instances where the jobseeker's perception of the job is not consistent with the actual job description. It is important for the job developer to advocate for the jobseeker as well as the employer so that the job is mutually beneficial. Sometimes jobseekers agree to job responsibilities that they have indicated in the M&G that they are not comfortable with or they can't perform.

The jobseeker should know that it's okay to turn down a job that's not right for them. Beyond26 will continue to search for the correct opportunity.

JOB COACHING

Job coaching is sometimes needed to allow a individual with a disability to be successful at a new job. Job coaches are offered as a tool to the employer as well as the employee to help allow that employee be successful. The degree and amount of coaching depends on the individual person and the job. While job coaching is a support that is provided during employment, the need for a job coach should be determined before seeking opportunities.

STEPS FOR SUPPORTIVE JOB COACHING*

1 THE JOB COACH MEETS THE JOBSEEKER PRIOR TO THE JOB START DATE

2 THE JOB COACH MEETS WITH THE EMPLOYER/MANAGER TO OBTAIN AND PROVIDE INFORMATION

3 THE JOB COACH SUPPORTS THE JOBSEEKER IN THEIR NEW POSITION

*FOR A COMPLETE, DETAILED BREAKDOWN OF STEPS PLEASE SEE APPENDIX G

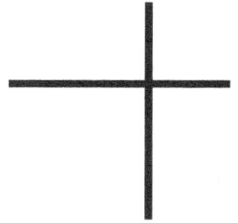

PROMOTING INDEPENDENCE

It's important to always remember that the ultimate goal of job coaching is to promote jobseeker independence. The job coach will always seek the least amount of support, deferring - as is possible - to natural support from fellow employees/on-the-job trainers.

Slowly, the job coach will assess the need and determine the degree of direct support as the jobseeker becomes more familiar and capable in their new role. In other words, if a jobseeker runs into a situation where they are unsure of what to do, the job coach would not want to immediately give them the answer. They would prompt the jobseeker, gradually, on how to reason through it or how to ask a coworker for help.

The goal is for the job coach to eventually not be needed on-site with the jobseeker. At this point, the job coach will provide off-site coaching, as needed, to discuss any further questions or concerns regarding their job.

JUST REMEMBER TO "TEACH, COACH, FADE"

TEACH: The job coach teaches the jobseeker steps required for the job (possibly including a job or task analysis)

COACH: The job coach steps back and coaches the jobseeker as needed

FADE: The job coach is available off-site for consulting and collaborative problem-solving with the employee/employer/manager

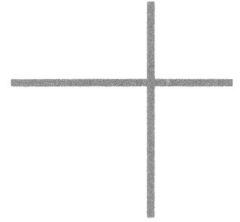

FINDING EMPLOYMENT

In this stage, the job developer will begin the task of finding and securing employment or volunteer positions for the jobseeker!

This section will detail (1) how to identify potential jobsites, (2) how to reach out to new business partners, and (3) how to support the jobseeker in securing employment when they decide to pursue an option.

From these steps, the following deliverables should be produced: (1) an updated jobseeker CRM record, (2) an updated check-in list, (3) an updated prayer list, (4) new business partner CRM record(s) if applicable.

IDENTIFYING POTENTIAL JOBSITES

When determining which businesses to reach out to, the job developer will want to consider all of the details provided in the jobseeker's profile. It's important to reflect on the jobseeker's interests while considering their necessary accommodations.

It is also a part of the mission to find a job that is in the jobseeker's community. The job developer should aim to find jobs that are close to the jobseeker's home in order to support the vision of "a community standing shoulder to shoulder."

REACHING OUT TO BUSINESSES

Reaching out to businesses is rewarding yet challenging. Be confident in the vision that jobseekers have a lot to offer their communities. Business partners are being offered dependable and enthusiastic employees who want to work! Reaching out to new businesses is a way of "proclaiming what we believe in such a way that we offer other people an opportunity to participate with us in our vision and mission."[5]

> You really have to look for what it is that's going to work, not only for the employer but also the employee.
>
> - Dirk Bakhuyzen, *Executive Director and Co-Founder*

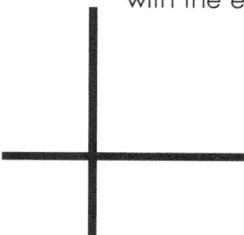

USING THE EXISTING NETWORK

Typically, the first step would be to review the existing network of business partners and see if there are any employers that align with the jobseeker's goals and abilities. If so, there should already be a point of contact.

If there are no businesses in the existing network that are a good fit for the jobseeker, the next step is to reach out to new businesses. A good place to start is to type the jobseeker's address into Google Maps and then identify nearby businesses that may be a good fit.

When a potential jobsite is identified, the first step should always be to ask the jobseeker if they would be interested in the job before approaching the employer. If the jobseeker is interested, a conversation can be initiated with the employer by following the method described in the next section.

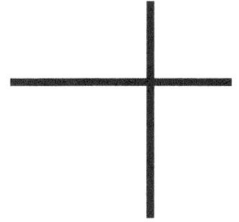

REACHING OUT FOR A JOBSEEKER

When reaching out to a new business, making an in-person visit is preferable. The job developer will stop in and ask if the business is currently hiring. If so, the job developer would then ask to speak to the person responsible for hiring or request their contact information.

From there, the job developer will provide the hiring personnel with a brief description of Beyond26 (including a brochure and business card) and a description of the jobseeker's abilities and accommodations. If the employer is interested, ask how they would prefer that the jobseeker apply.

EXPANDING THE NETWORK OF BUSINESS PARTNERS

When possible, the job developer should be continually working on expanding the business partner network, so that they are able to refer jobseekers as applicable. For that reason, it's good to reach out to local businesses proactively on an ongoing basis.

> With the help of the job coaches and the employees that they send us, it's been nothing but a positive experience.
>
> - Mike Stanford, *Business Partner*

When reaching out proactively, the job developer can use the letter in Appx H and customize as needed to email or drop by and hand-deliver (preferred method) to local businesses. Make sure to bring a brochure and ask for the owner or manager's business card when possible.

Then, the job developer will follow up via phone or email to thank the individual for their time or confirm that they received the information if they were unavailable. The job developer will answer any questions and add the business to the CRM if applicable.

SECURING EMPLOYMENT

If the jobseeker and employer are both interested, the jobseeker will complete an application (with the job developer's assistance if necessary) and the profile and resume should be forwarded to the employer.

Next, the job developer should set up a time for the jobseeker to view the facility and to interview. If the job or volunteer position is offered and if the jobseeker and/or the employer prefers, the jobseeker may do a 1-2 day unpaid job shadow to find if they are a good fit. If the job shadow does not work, the job developer will continue the search and repeat the process.

If the job shadow was a success, the job developer may wish to conduct a "warm hand-off" - a conversation between the jobseeker and the employer to verify job details and confirm that both parties' needs will be met. This meeting will determine a start date and determine what the jobseeker needs to do before the start date.

Then, complete the steps in the "Employed Jobseeker Action Plan." See Appx I for a compiled checklist.

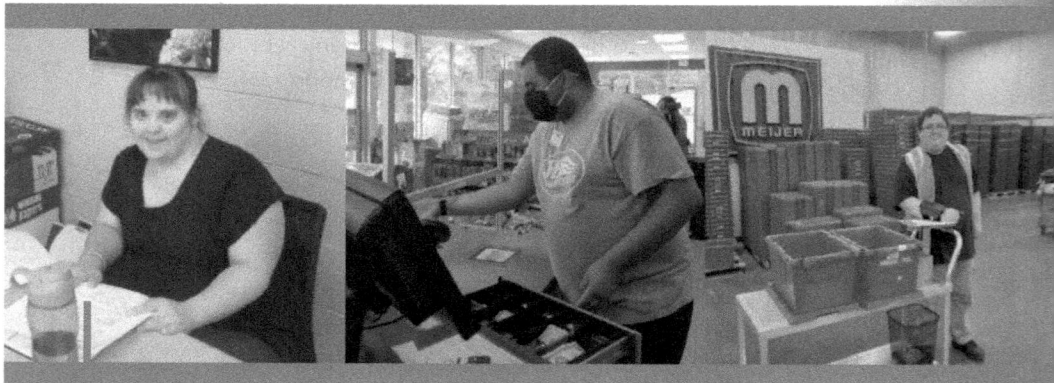

EMPLOYED JOBSEEKER ACTION PLAN

Before the start date, the job developer will make sure that the jobseeker gets proper clothing and fills out all necessary paperwork. Finally, they will complete the following:

1 CHANGE JOBSEEKER'S CRM RECORD:
- SWITCH STATUS IN CRM TO *EMPLOYED*
- ADD HIRE DATE, PLACE OF EMPLOYMENT, MANAGER'S CONTACT INFORMATION, AND SCHEDULE (IF REGULAR)

2 ADD BUSINESS TO CRM (IF NEW) AND UPDATE STATUS

3 ADD NEWLY EMPLOYED JOBSEEKER TO CHECK-IN LIST AND UPDATE PRAYER LIST

4 MAKE SURE BUSINESS HAS RECEIVED A THANK YOU EMAIL AND DIGITAL FLYER WITH CONTACTS (SEE PG 28)

POST-EMPLOYMENT SERVICES

The purpose of the post-employment services is to provide support after the jobseeker is hired, in order to ensure that the jobseeker feels comfortable and equipped to handle any issues that may arise. Many jobseekers have difficulty advocating for themselves and letting their employer know when accommodations need to be made, so some may feel like they need to quit the job. It's important that they know we are here to support them every step of the way

It is equally important to make sure that the business partner feels comfortable to voice any questions or concerns that they may have. We want our employers to see our jobseekers as an asset, so we need to make sure that our jobseeker is meeting their needs as a business. We also want to make sure that the employer knows that we appreciate their partnership!

All of this can be accomplished by consistent and open post-employment communication. This section will provide guidance on how to ensure that all parties needs are being met by performing: (1) jobseeker check-ins and (2) business partner check-ins. From these steps, a jobseeker check-in list should be produced.

> [Our employed jobseeker] works hard and always has a positive attitude. She is courteous with the customers. She has been a great addition to our store. Beyond26 is so easy to work with.
>
> - Betsy, *Business Partner*

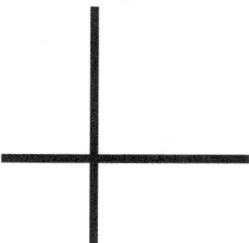

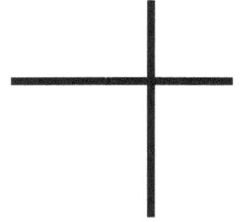

JOBSEEKER CHECK-INS

WHAT TO ADDRESS

1. How is your job working out for you?
2. Are there any areas of concern?
3. Are there any positive experiences that you want to share with us?
4. How can we can support you further?

TRACKING CHECK-INS

Frequency of check-ins can vary based on the jobseeker's individual needs, but as a general rule the job developer will want to attempt to check-in with the jobseeker or jobseeker's primary contact:

* Immediately after the first shift
* Again after 1-2 weeks
* On a monthly basis from there on out OR as requested

Some jobseekers may request that the job developer check-in more frequently than once a month and some may not want check-ins at all. Just ask the jobseeker at the second check-in what they would prefer and let them know that they can always reach out if they want to!

The job developer is responsible for maintaining a spreadsheet to track check-ins. The spreadsheet should provide a system for indicating which jobseekers need check-ins and how frequently they need to be performed. The job developer should also record any feedback (positive or negative) in the jobseekers' CRM records.

BUSINESS PARTNER CHECK-INS

WHAT TO ADDRESS

1. How has [jobseeker] been doing at their job?
2. Are there any areas of concern?
3. Is there anything that you would like us to work on with [jobseeker]?
4. Are there any positive experiences that you want to share with us?

Check-ins with business partners are usually conducted once per jobseeker, after about a week (or 3-4 shifts), and unless a business partner indicates otherwise, ongoing check-ins are not necessary. The job developer should make it known that the business partner can reach out at any time with any concerns.

THANKING BUSINESS PARTNERS

After a business hires a jobseeker, the job developer should send a "Thank You" email and attach a digital flyer with Beyond26 contacts as soon as possible (See pg 28).

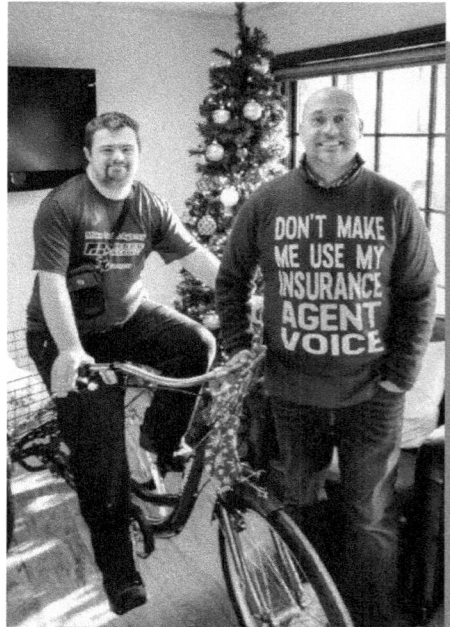

All interactions with business partners should be recorded in the CRM. Typically, one specifically assigned Beyond26 team member will want to serve as the point of contact for each business partner to prevent confusion or miscommunication.

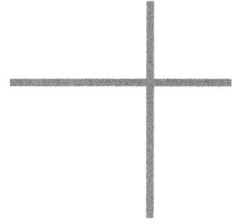

CONCLUSION

It may seem that the main beneficiary is the employed jobseeker, however the benefits of inclusivity spread to those around the jobseekers as well. Employment positively impacts the jobseekers' caregivers who get to see their loved one thrive, as well as the businesses that they work for who gain a dependable employee.

The community as a whole benefits when they see individuals with disabilities successfully and enthusiastically performing their job duties as well. Not only is a happy employee a pleasure to clientele, but it often reduces stigma and inspires community members to do their part to embrace individuals with disabilities in their own businesses and communities. At the end of the day, it's all about creating opportunities for individuals with disabilities and the best way to do so is through visibility.

> [Our employed jobseeker] has been a godsend to our team... She's a hard worker that pushes past her own comfort zone and amazes me daily.
>
> - Bonnie, *Business Partner*

REFERENCES

[1] Collaborative on Faith and Disabilities. *Putting Faith to Work*. Vanderbilt Kennedy Center, 2016.

[2] Open Systems Healthcare. (2019, October 8). What Makes a Successful DSP?. Open Systems Healthcare. https://opensystemshealthcare.com/what-makes-a-successful-dsp/

[3] 13 On Your Side. (2020, March 11). 'Exploring Beyond26' gives new purpose to people with disabilities in West Michigan [Video]. https://www.wzzm13.com/article/news/local/exploring-beyond26-employment-event/69-e4da7523-00e5-4f4f-8858-144ecc1153aa

[4] DeJong, J. (Host). (2019–2020). Infinity and Beyond26 [Audio podcast]. WKTV Journal. https://www.wktvjournal.org/podcast/infinity-and-beyond-26/

[5] Nouwen, Henri. A *Spirituality of Fundraising*. Upper Room Books, 2011.

> [Our employed jobseekers] are a joy to work with. I can't say enough about the work ethic that both of them have. It's just been a really good fit.
>
> - Seth, *Business Partner*

APPENDICES

Downloadable blank versions and sample completed versions of all appendix itemscan be found in the Google Drive folder titled "Support Team Resources," along with the following documents:

- Beyond26 brochure
- Sample Meet & Greet flyer
- Release of Information (ROI) form
- Jobseeker Advocate Action Plan
- Sample Prayer List
- Business Partner "Thank You" Flyer

APPENDIX A

Beyond26 Meet & Greet Action Plan (Check-list)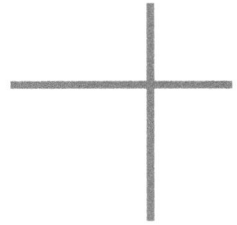

	Preparing for the Meet & Greet Session
	1. **Contact/Connect** with jobseeker by phone or email: Arrange for meeting time for the Meet & Greet. Get basic information on the jobseeker (first and last name, phone #, email)
	2. **Add Jobseeker and Enter Information** into Less Annoying CRM under Jobseeker Pipeline and update status to Active (Save information each time)
	3. **Reserve** room or site to have the Meet & Greet session
	4. **Send Reminder Email** to jobseeker one day prior to Meet & Greet session
	Meet & Greet Session
	1. **Prepare Materials** • Beyond26 pamphlet, flyer, release of information form, copy of jobseeker question guide, and copy of interviewer question guide • computer is available for the intake specialist • bottled water is handy
	2. **Listen** to hopes and dreams of the jobseeker • Using the Question Guide for the Interviewer, fill out basic information (take photo of jobseeker and obtain signature on release of information form) • Discuss possibilities of jobs and sites
	Follow up for Meet & Greet Session
	1. **Discuss** job possibilities with Job Developer or Jobseeker Advocate
	2. **Complete and Share Profile/Resume with:** • Job Developer or Jobseeker Advocate & Executive Director, pertinent staff • Jobseeker (NOTE: make a digital copy and share only pgs. 1 & 2), ask jobseeker if there are any needed edits
	3. **Make Copies of Profile/Resume**: One complete hard copy placed in a new file in our file cabinet Profile/resume web address added to the jobseeker's CRM contact form
	4. **Fill out CRM Completely** using the info from the profile • Subscribe jobseeker and caregiver to email list and caregiver to mailing list • Update the jobseeker's status in the CRM to *Application/Meet & Greet Completed* (along with Priority level)
	5. **Update** Prayer List with newest jobseeker

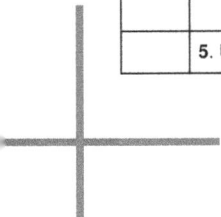

APPENDIX B

Skills I bring to a job:	**Jimmy Smith's Profile**	Supports that help my success:
• • • • • • My prior work experience: • • •	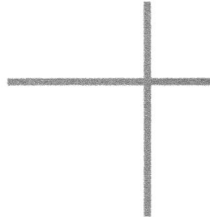 How people describe me: Contact Information:	• • • • • • • • • • •
Paid or volunteer work: Type of work preferred: Type of work not preferred: Community preferred: Possible Locations for jobs:	**D.O.B:** Address: Phone#: Email Address: Primary Contact: Phone#: Email Address: **Primary** Contacts **Address:**	Transportation: Total hours/week: Days preferred: Amount of hours/day: Time of day preferred: Amount of pay: Start date:

Beyond26
Address
www.beyondtwentysix.org - Phone

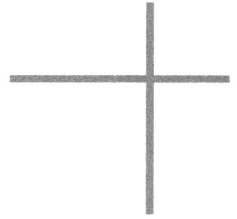

APPENDIX C

Name

Address | Phone Number | Email

OBJECTIVE: Seeking a (list type of position desired) using my (list experience) to further the mission of (company mission) for (company name).

EXPERIENCE:

Title (Company)   MM/YY- MM/YY
    Description

Title (Company)   MM/YY- MM/YY
    Description

EDUCATION:

Name of College/Vocational training (if applicable)   (YYYY Graduated)
    List any honors/achievements

Name of High School   (YYYY Graduated)
    List any honors/achievements

SKILLS:

- List any hard skills

APPENDIX D
Question Guide for Beyond26 Interviewer

Welcome jobseeker and ask if there are any questions about Beyond26. Reassure the jobseeker that this is not an interview but just a "getting-to-know-you" session.
Confirm Jobseeker's Name/D.O.B./Address/Phone#/Email/Picture
 Primary or Emergency Contact's Name/Address/Phone#/Email

1. Tell us about yourself:

- What do you enjoy doing for fun at home or in the community?
 Ex: I like_____ ___, I enjoy_____
- What special interests, gifts, passions, hobbies do you have? What do you love to talk about with people?
 Ex: My hobby is_____ My real interest(s) is/are_____
- How would people who know you describe you?
 Ex: kind, friendly, outgoing, prefer a few people at a time

2. What skills do you bring to the job?

- What do you consider to be some of your strengths?
 (What strengths have other people noticed in you? Everyone has gifts, talents, and qualities that can benefit a business. What gifts/talents would a potential employer want to know about you? What are you really good at or becoming good at?)
 Ex: Dependable, on-time, friendly, get along with others, team player, can focus on task at hand, willing to follow routines, can read directions, writing/reading skills, positive attitude, helpful, hard worker, flexible

3. What prior work experiences have you had?

- What volunteer or paid jobs have you had in the past? (in school, the community, in a church, responsibilities at home)
- Is there someone we could talk to who could tell us more or be a reference?

4. Job Interests *(Is there something you feel "called to do?")*

- What types of jobs do you think would be really interesting? What did you enjoy doing in your past jobs? If looking for volunteer opportunities...are there things in the community you enjoy doing that would make a great job? What types of job responsibilities would be a really good fit for you?
- What types of job responsibilities should you definitely avoid? What did you not like about past jobs?
- Think about the following features of a job:
 *Community Location of your job: do you want to be close to home/community?
 *Do you know of any possible job locations?
 *What type of transportation do you have?

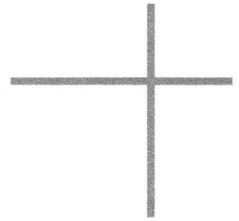

APPENDIX D (CONT.)

*Days/hours preferred? Number of hours to work in a week?
*Social nature of job?
*Amount of pay?
*Start date?

5. How can an employer offer support for your success?
(Do not limit options. The right support can be found for many jobs.)

Let's talk about what would help you be most successful finding and keeping a job. Were there any supports in past jobs that helped you be successful? Whichof the following supports do you think you will need?
- Assist in developing a resume or one-page profile
- Assist in finding a job and encouragement through the job search
- Practicing for an interview
- Job Shadow: Pre-job training/practice to learn job skills
- Provide initial job coach
- Provide long-term job coach
- Periodic check-ins by Beyond26 or a coach/mentor to keep the job over longer period of time
- Extra employer training so they know how best to support you
- Provide written schedule of the work day
- Provide a checklist of specific tasks I need to complete
- Provide verbal, written, and/or hands-on directions as well
- Demonstrate new tasks
- Demonstrate new tasks by breaking up job skills into steps (task analysis)
- Tell me schedule/job changes ahead of time so that I can prepare
- Have accessible staff available to answer questions as they arise (go-to person)
- Allow time to complete tasks
- Allow use of a water bottle
- Other Accommodations or changes to a job related to a possible disability (break time, standing, sitting, service dogs, weight limit, word font, etc.)

6. Do you receive any public support that could be affected by or assist in a job?

- SSDI/SSI (if so, do you wish to keep your full benefits?)
- Medicare/Medicaid (if so, do you wish to keep your full benefits?)
- CLS support or other support (# of hours, can these hours be used to support you in a job?)

7. **Don't forget to ask about picture** and ROI form

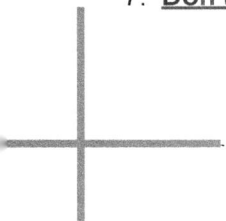

APPENDIX E

Question Guide for Beyond26 Jobseeker

Job Seeker's Name:
Date of Birth:
Address:
Phone/Email:
Primary or Emergency Contact's Name:
Primary Contact's Phone/Email:
Primary Contact's Address:

1. Tell us about yourself:

   - What do you enjoy doing for fun at home or in the community?
     Ex: I like _____, I enjoy_____
   - What special interests, gifts, passions, hobbies do you have? What do you love to talk about with people?
     Ex: My hobby is_____ My real interest(s) is/are_____
   - How would people who know you describe you?
     Ex: kind, friendly, outgoing, prefer a few people at a time

2. What skills do you bring to the job?

   - What do you consider to be some of your strengths?
     Ex: Dependable, on-time, friendly, get along with others, team player, can focus on task at hand, willing to follow routines, can read directions, writing/reading skills, positive attitude, helpful, hard worker, flexible

3. What prior work-related experiences have you had?

   - What volunteer or paid jobs have you had in the past? (in school, the community, in a church, responsibilities at home)

4. Job Interests *(Is there something you feel "called" to do?)*

   - What types of jobs do you think would be really interesting?
   - What types of job responsibilities should you definitely avoid?

5. How can an employer support for your success?
   (Do not limit options. The right support can be found for many jobs.)

Let's talk about what would help you be most successful finding and keeping a job. Were there any supports in past jobs that helped you be successful? Which of the following supports do you think you will need?
   - Assist in developing a resume or one-page profile
   - Assist in finding a job and encouragement through the job search
   - Practicing for an interview

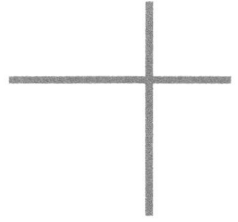

APPENDIX E (CONT.)

- Job Shadow: Pre-job training/practice to learn job skills
- Provide initial job coach
- Provide long-term job coach
- Periodic check-ins by Beyond26 or a coach/mentor to keep the job over longer period of time
- Extra employer training so they know how best to support you
- Provide written schedule of the work day
- Provide a checklist of specific tasks I need to complete
- Provide verbal, written, &/or hands-on directions as well
- Demonstrate new tasks
- Demonstrate new tasks by breaking up job skills into steps (task analysis)
- Tell me schedule {job changes ahead of time so that I can prepare
- Have accessible staff available to answer questions as they arise (go-to person)
- Allow time to complete tasks
- Be willing to listen
- Allow use of a water bottle
- Other Accommodations or changes to a job related to a possible disability (break time, standing, signing, service dogs, weight limit, word font, etc.)

6. Do you receive any public support that could be affected by or assist in a job?

- SSDI/SSI (if so, do you wish to keep your full benefits?)
- Medicare/Medicaid (if so, do you wish to keep your full benefits?)
- CLS support or other support {# of hours, can these hours be used to support you in a job?)

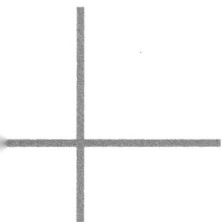

APPENDIX F

Beyond26

Jimmy Smith's Profile

How people describe me:
Caring, Easy to get along with, perceptive, friendly, helpful

Contact Information:

D.O.B: 10/25/1998
Address: 345 W. Elm St, Hudsonville MI
Phone #: 616-433-4958
Email Address: email@gmail.com
Primary Contact: Steve Smith (Dad)
Phone #: 616-837-4947
Email Address: email@gmail.com
Primary Contacts Address: 3910 62nd St SE, Wyoming MI

Skills I bring to a job:
- Hard Worker
- Team Player
- Can stay on track
- Can follow routines with a list
- Can read basic instructions
- Can do basic math
- Can figure out money
- Positive Attitude
- Prefers to stick to the routine

My prior work experience:
- **B26 Document Shredding**
- **J&H Family Stores-** cleaning/ stocking
- **Panera Bread-** cleaning
- **Surefil-** assembly/ packaging

Paid or volunteer work: preferably paid but will do either one
Type of work preferred: cleaning, cutting grass, weed whacking, leaf blowing, stocking shelves, dusting, washing cars, shovelling snow
Type of work not preferred: clean bathrooms, wash dishes
Community preferred: Grandville area
Possible Locations for jobs: not sure

Supports that help my success:
- Assist in developing a resume
- Assist in finding job
- Practice for an interview
- Job Shadow first
- Provide initial job coach
- Provide long-term job coach
- Periodic checks by Beyond 26
- Employer training
- Provide written schedule of the work day.
- Provide a checklist of specific tasks to be completed
- Provide verbal/written/hands-on directions
- Demonstrate new tasks
- Demonstrate new tasks by breaking up skills into steps(task analysis)
- Tell me schedule/job changes ahead of time so that I can prepare
- Provide an accessible staff member (a go-to person)
- Allow time to complete tasks
- Be willing to listen
- Allow use of a water bottle

Transportation: parents, bike
Total hours/week: 20 hours paid, Volunteer up to full-time
Days preferred: Monday-Saturday
Amount of hours/day: up to 8
Time of day preferred: daytime/evening
Amount of pay: minimum
Start date: ASAP

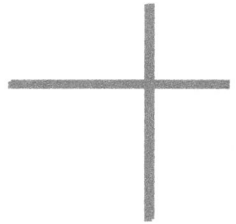

APPENDIX G

> Beyond26
>
> ### TIPS AND STEPS FOR the JOB COACH
>
> Job coaching is often needed to **allow an individual with a disability to be successful at a new job**. Job coaches are offered as a tool to the employer to help that employee be successful. The degree and amount depends on the individual person and the job. Job coaching actually begins before a jobseeker's first day on the job with the **ultimate goal of striving towards jobseeker independence**. In order to do that, the job coach will progress from fulltime on the job site teaching & coaching to facilitate learning...transitioning to fading off site consulting for collaborative problem solving .

Job Coach Action Plan

1.	**The job coach meets the jobseeker:**
	1. Attend Meet & Greet session with job development team if possible
	2. Meet with jobseeker before job begins in a "neutral" setting to establish rapport, determine what the jobseeker knows, answer questions, share an overview of the job, discuss safety considerations, etc.
2.	**The job coach meets with the employer/manager (if necessary) to obtain the following:**
	1. Written job description/work schedule
	2. New employee handbook/policies/procedures
	3. Training protocol
	4. Date & times to report for training/contact person upon arrival
	5. Supervisor name & contact info
	6. List of items for employee to bring on 1st day (ex:documentation, ID, name tag, uniform)
	The job coach provides information to employer: **(Get permission from jobseeker to share information with employer)**
	1. Information about communication styles of the jobseeker and supports to allow the jobseeker to be successful (identified in jobseeker profile)
	2. Information about the job coach role
	a. Description given of job coach's role and responsibility: Teach, Coach, and Fade
	c. Names and contact information of job coach given to employer
	3. Ask if employer has any questions

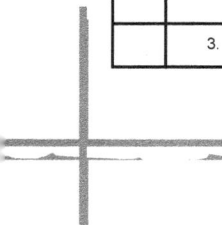

APPENDIX G (CONT.)

3.	**The job coach supports the employee**
	a. Complete Worksite Analysis if necessary (completed before job start date)
	1. View job if possible ahead of time/video record a current employee completing the task &/or takepictures of workplace/tasks
	2. Identify & record potential barriers and possible adaptations that would be useful... discuss these with employer.
	b. Job Analysis (Teach ⟹ Coach)
	1. List of required tasks (Use pictures, picture & words, or words only...or move from pictures &words to words only, flip book/binder, check list)
	2. Assemble materials needed
	3. Identify possible needed adaptations
	c. Task Analysis (Teach ⟹ Coach)
	1. Steps required for each task required on the job
	2. Record on a checklist, notebook, or iPad.
	3. Start with many steps/ collapse steps gradually
	d. Teaching multiple tasks (Teach ⟹ Coach ⟹ Fade)
	1. Model steps of each job task
	2. Determine lowest level of prompting or support
	3. Document level of support needed to avoid over supporting employee
	e. Encouraging natural support workplace communication (Coach ⟹ Fade)
	1. Encourage employee to communicate directly with coworkers or supervisor
	2. Job coach models effective ways to speak and communicate to coworkers
	f. Step back from direct teaching and coaching (Fade)
	1. Step back from the direct coaching
	2. Spend time in the environment only observing
	3. Be available off-site for consulting and collaborative problem-solving for employer/employee

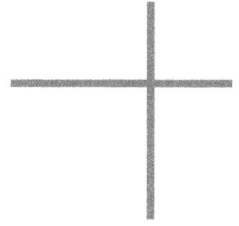

APPENDIX H

DATE

Business Name
Address
City, State ZIP

Beyond26

Dear [Community Partner],

I am reaching out to you on behalf of Beyond26. We are a local nonprofit that helps individuals with disabilities find employment. The purpose of this letter is to see if, in the future, you would be open to hiring one of our jobseekers if a qualified candidate came along.

Beyond26 is a unique organization because we serve individuals with disabilities ranging from Down Syndrome to Autism to hearing impairments. Many of these disabilities don't affect the performance of specific jobs - it's just about linking our jobseekers up with jobs that are appropriate for them. That's where we would love your support! Because we try to match up jobseekers based on their skill set and interests, we typically cultivate business partners first, and then refer jobseekers as applicable.

So, being a business partner with us would look something like this:

If we have a jobseeker that we feel would be a good fit for your company (whether it's volunteer or paid), we will reach out and send you their profile and resume to review and determine if you feel they would be a good fit. Likewise, if you have an open position at your company you could reach out to Beyond26, and we can send you any candidates that we may have.

Other local business partners include [list other prominent partners here]. Our business partners tend to describe our jobseekers as dependable, enthusiastic, and upbeat employees. These are individuals who want to work and are eager to join their community as valued members of a work environment.

Meijer has reported that our jobseekers are, "a joy to work with – very eager to do a great job, asking for feedback – I can't say enough about the work ethic that [they] have. It's just been a really good fit."

For our jobseekers, the benefit is clear. "I love [my] job. It's amazing. It helps me achieve my goals and makes me proud and continue to work hard... and make myself happier," said our employed jobseeker of his placement at a local J&H Family Store.

If you're interested in hiring employees who want to work, we would be happy to have [business name] as a partner! I have included a copy of our brochure for you to review and get more information about our mission and our goal. If you have any other questions, please feel free to reach out. Thank you for your time, and I hope to hear from you soon!

Sincerely,

[Signature]
Name
Job Developer

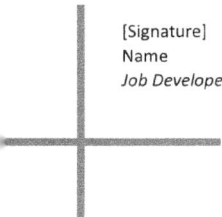

APPENDIX I

Beyond26 Employed Jobseeker (New Hire) Action Plan

Putting Faith to Work... Shoulder to Shoulder

1. Change jobseeker's info on the CRM: 1) status on the CRM to Employed On-Site/Off Site 2) place of employment 3) manager's contact info 4) hire date 5) hours working (if regular) 6) days working (if regular)
2. Add business (if new) to Business Pipeline and update status
3. Add newly employed jobseeker to Jobseeker Check-In list
4. Update information on the prayer list with hire date and business
5. Maintain contact with new hiree and employer as needed on the Jobseeker Check-In List
6. Send business a Thank You email and digital flyer with Beyond26 contacts (Share "Thank you/Information Flyer for employer") if appropriate
7. Email Beyond26 team about new hiree to celebrate

www.beyondtwentysix.org

REACH US

A 4340 BURLINGAME AVE SW
WYOMING, MI 49509

T (616) 884-6400

W WWW.BEYONDTWENTYSIX.ORG
E DBAKHUYZEN@BEYONDTWENTYSIX.ORG

www.ingramcontent.com/pod-product-compliance
Lightning Source LLC
Chambersburg PA
CBHW060244030426
42335CB00014B/1593